A Naturalist's Guide to

Garden Wildlife

Marianne Taylor

BEAUFOY BOOKS

First published in the United Kingdom in 2010 by Beaufoy Books
11 Blenheim Court, 316 Woodstock Road, Oxford OX2 7NS, England
www.johnbeaufoy.com

10 9 8 7 6 5 4 3 2

ISBN 978-1-906780-14-2

PICTURE CREDITS

Front cover: *top left* Great Spotted Woodpecker, male; *top right* Peacock;
bottom left Yellow Iris; *bottom middle* Grey Squirrel; *bottom right* Common
Frog. **Back cover:** Garden Tiger. **Title page:** Bullfinch, male. **Contents
page:** Common Dog-violet. All by Paul Sterry.
Main descriptions: all photographs by Paul Sterry except for the following,
which were supplied by Nature Photographers Ltd:
Frank Blackburn 19(top); Andy Callow 100(top); Colin Carver
47(bottom); Andrew Cleave 48(top), 131(bottom), 150(top); Geoff du
Feu 42(top), 89(bottom), 93(top), 94(bottom); Ernie Janes 45(bottom),
48(bottom); Andrew Merrick 43(bottom), 54(top); Lee Morgan 49(top);
Owen Newman 41(bottom); Richard Revels 46(bottom), 53(bottom),
92(top), 96(bottom); EK Thompson 18(top).

Edited, designed and typeset by
D & N Publishing, Baydon, Wiltshire, UK

Printed and bound in Malaysia by Times Offset (M) Sdn. Bhd.

·Contents·

INTRODUCTION

In Britain, many of us are in the fortunate position of having an area of outside space that we can call our own – a garden. More and more people now appreciate their gardens not only as extensions to the home, to be planned and decorated as they wish, but as miniature personal wildernesses where wildlife can be encouraged and enjoyed.

The layout of the average town is such that gardens, though sometimes small individually, combine to form substantial patches of varied wildlife habitat, providing a substitute for the open countryside they have replaced. Many species of plants and animals that traditionally live in woodland or meadowland are now more familiar to us as garden inhabitants. Rural homes with extensive gardens that are allowed to 'run wild' here and there can boast a list of species rivalling that of many a nature reserve.

Even a small urban garden can attract a good range of species. Birds, with their unrivalled powers of travel, will visit even the tiniest backyard if there is food (natural or provided on a bird table) to attract them. A small patch of soil left unplanted will soon be colonised by those pioneer wild plants we often dismiss as 'weeds', but that include some of the most attractive species you'll see anywhere. If your garden is blessed with a tree or two and a pond, you can expect the diversity of species to increase even further.

A colourful herbaceous border need not hold only exotic garden flowers – mix in some native species to attract more wildlife.

Walls cloaked in Ivy provide shelter for nesting birds, and the Ivy flowers are a valuable late-autumn nectar source for insects.

Enjoying Your Garden Wildlife

The biggest problem for wildlife as far as gardens are concerned is the large proportion of non-native plant species that many of us cultivate, as we find their blooms and foliage showier and more impressive than home-grown species. Our native insects have co-evolved with our native plants, so it is hardly surprising that caterpillars have not yet adapted to eat the foliage of garden plants brought in from the other side of the world. To make your garden a friendlier place for wildlife, sow native plant seeds (or leave a space for them and wait for them to colonise it naturally), and if you have a native tree growing in your space, cherish it. The Pedunculate Oak, for example, has nearly 300 species of insects associated with it, which in turn will enable their predators – including other insects, birds and small mammals – to flourish.

If you have an area of lawn, try leaving a section uncut through the summer. You may be surprised at how many new wild flowers appear, which in turn will attract butterflies, moths, hoverflies and bees. Other helpful additions you can make to your garden include woodpiles (ideal for beetle larvae and hibernating Hedgehogs) and ponds – even an upturned dustbin lid sunk in the soil can develop a miniature aquatic ecosystem that will help boost your garden's overall attractiveness to wildlife.

Getting to know the wildlife in your garden doesn't require much in the way of additional equipment. Binoculars will give you a better look at birds, mammals and large insects, while a hand lens is a very affordable and rewarding tool for examining smaller insects and details on plants. If you enjoy photography, you will gain much from documenting your garden wildlife this way, and the simplest of notebooks will suffice for recording observations.

Further investigations you might consider include using a light trap to attract and catch moths, for identification and then release; using a bat detector to analyse the calls of any bat species that are active in your area; making spore prints from mushrooms to determine spore colour (just leave a mushroom cap on a sheet of white or coloured paper for a couple of hours); and using simple pit-fall traps to study the ground-dwelling insects and other 'mini-beasts' roaming the undergrowth.

LEFT: *Many species of moths (this is a Large Yellow Underwing) are attracted to outside lights at night, and may rest nearby the next day.*

OPPOSITE PAGE: *Peanuts contain plenty of fat and protein. Providing foods like this will help small birds, like Siskins and Blue Tits seen here, survive a hard winter.*

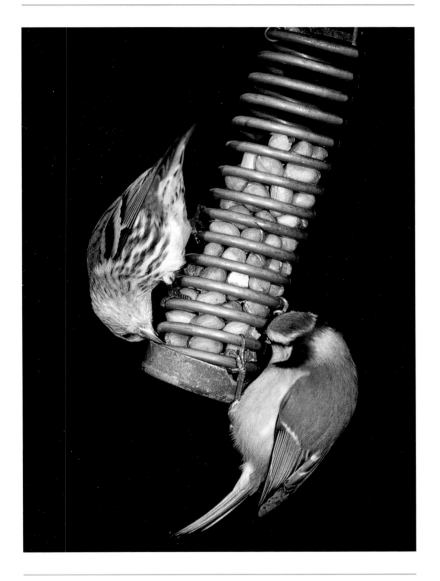

RIGHT: *A typical nestbox designed for small songbirds. The hole diameter can be adjusted to attract different species, for example 2.5cm for Blue Tits, 2.8cm for Great Tits and 3.2cm for House Sparrows.*

BELOW: *Many native wild flowers, like the Viper's Bugloss, are both beautiful and rich nectar sources, attracting bumblebees and other insects.*

Many of us enjoy feeding garden birds. Providing scraps on the lawn or a simple bird table is an easy way to attract species like thrushes, tits and finches. If this really becomes a passion, you can buy an array of birdfeeders and dispense everything from shelled sunflower seeds and suet balls to live, wriggling mealworms. Nestboxes provide a substitute for natural tree-holes and can entice tits, Robins, Starlings and sparrows to breed in your garden; specialist nestboxes are also available for species like Swifts, House Martins and Tawny Owls. In addition, there is an increasing range of products available to attract other animals, such as 'toad homes', where toads can hibernate; 'mini-beast hotels', offering sheltered winter accommodation for insects like lacewings; and 'bumblebee homes' to encourage these insects to establish breeding colonies.

About this Book

With its concise and detailed descriptions and clear photographs, this guide will enable you to identify the majority of animal, plant and fungus species that will be encountered in the average northwestern European garden. Inevitably, surprises will appear from time to time – in some gardens more than others, with coastal and very rural gardens the likeliest to produce the unexpected. Just as inevitably, an interest in wildlife that begins in your garden is likely to take you to many other places where you can observe a wider variety of species. The References and Further Reading section on p. 156 recommends some books that will enable you to explore the wider world of nature.

How to Use this Book

The garden wildlife species described in this book are organised into conventional groupings. The guide begins with birds, then goes on to describe other vertebrates, followed by insects and other invertebrates. Next, the book covers trees and herbaceous plants, and finishes with mosses and fungi.

Each species account is structured in essentially the same way. The heading gives the species' common English name, scientific name and size. The size is qualified with the type of measurement (wingspan, length, etc.) where clarification is necessary. In animals, size always refers to adult individuals. In plants, size varies greatly according to age, so the figure given is a normal maximum. Units used are metres for measurements of 2m or more, centimetres for measurements of 1–199cm, and millimetres for measurements of less than 1cm/10mm. Bird photographs are of adult males, where there is a difference between the sexes, unless specified otherwise.

The species accounts are each divided into three main sections. The first is a DESCRIPTION of the species, including any differences between the sexes and adult and juvenile forms, descriptions of the early stages in invertebrates, and a detailed look at the different parts in plants. The second section covers DISTRIBUTION, and gives a brief overview of the species' range in northwestern Europe. The final section is HABITS AND HABITAT in animals, and LIFE CYCLE AND HABITAT in plants and fungi. It gives some background biology to the species concerned, describing behaviour in animals, the life stages in invertebrates, and flowering seasons in plants. While habitat can be assumed to include gardens in all cases, a little more detail is provided in terms of the species' general habitat preferences – soil type and shade for plants, preferred plant species to be present for insects, and so on. General flying seasons for insects and flowering seasons for plants are given in this section – please note that in the far north these periods may be shortened. For example, flowers that bloom from March in southern England may not appear until May in northern Sweden.

Springtime means the chance to observe exciting breeding behaviour, such as courtship feeding between pairs of Robins.

Glossary

Every effort has been made to avoid the use of unfamiliar terminology and jargon in this book. However, to maintain the concise structure of the species accounts, it has sometimes been necessary to use certain words and phrases that may not be known to all readers. Full explanations of these words and phrases are given below. In addition, diagrams indicating the parts of a flower and parts of a bird are also included below to aid identification.

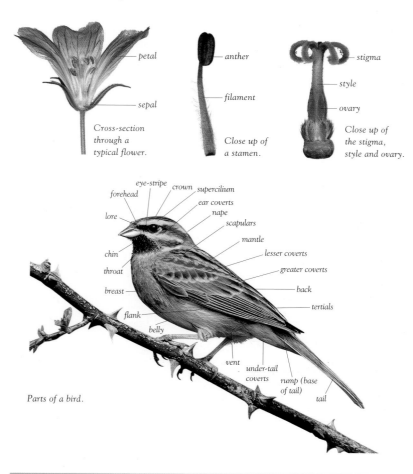

petal

anther

stigma

filament

style

ovary

sepal

Cross-section through a typical flower.

Close up of a stamen.

Close up of the stigma, style and ovary.

eye-stripe   crown   supercilium

forehead

ear coverts

nape

lore

scapulars

mantle

chin

lesser coverts

throat

greater coverts

breast

back

flank

tertials

belly

vent

under-tail coverts

rump (base of tail)

tail

Parts of a bird.

Abdomen The third of the three body sections in insects, the second of the two in spiders.

Annual A plant that lives for one year, producing seed that establishes the new generation the following year.

Antennae Sensory appendages on the heads of insects and some other invertebrates; usually long, fine and mobile.

Barring Of animal patterning, describes fine stripes that run across the body rather than along it.

Bask To rest in sunshine in order to raise the body temperature.

Batesian mimic A harmless species that has evolved to resemble another that is harmful – e.g. that is poisonous, distasteful or carries a sting. The harmless species benefits as it is not attacked by predators, which have learned to avoid the dangerous species it mimics.

Biennial A plant that lives for two years, producing seed in its second year.

Bill In birds, another word for the beak.

Bract In plants, a specialised leaf closely associated with a flower.

Cephalothorax The combined head and thorax body section in spiders.

Cere In birds, an area of waxy bare skin, sometimes raised, at the base of the top mandible of the bill.

Cocoon A silky ball produced by some insects and spiders, inside which a larva pupates or a spider's eggs are protected.

Complete metamorphosis In insects, to pass through four distinct physical stages: egg, larva, pupa, adult. Occurs in beetles, butterflies, bees and others.

Composite flower head A cluster of florets, which together create a distinct form that has the appearance of a single flower, e.g. a Daisy.

Corolla The tubular part of a flower, formed where the petals fuse at the base. May be short or long.

Crest A raised tuft of feathers on the head of a bird; a ridge of skin on a newt's back; raised hairs on an insect's thorax.

Crustaceans The animal group containing crabs, shrimps and woodlice.

Cuticle The outer casing of an insect or other invertebrate, which in some cases is regularly moulted and replaced.

Deciduous A perennial plant that sheds its leaves in autumn and is leafless until the following spring.

Echolocaton The navigation system of bats, in which the echoes of their squeaking calls enable them to build a 'sound map' of their surroundings.

Evergreen A plant that retains its leaves throughout the year.

Eye-stripe In birds, a dark marking running from the base of the bill to the back of the head, along the same plane as the eye.

Fissure A narrow, long crack or indentation in tree bark or other hard surface.

Flight feathers The long outer feathers in a bird's wing.

Floret A tiny flower, many of which collectively form a composite flower head.

Flower head/spike A rounded/pointed cluster of flowers.

Foliage The leaves of a plant.

Foodplant The plant species that is eaten by a given insect larva – e.g. Stinging Nettle is the foodplant of the Small Tortoiseshell butterfly.

Gall A swelling in part of a plant, caused by a burrowing insect larva.

Generation In insects, one complete breeding cycle from egg to adult.

Grazing Of mammals and birds, eating grass.

Gregarious Sociable, inclined to gather with others of its own species or other similar species.

Habitat The environment occupied by any given species.

Herbaceous plant A plant with leaves and stems that die down after the growing season (although in perennials, underground parts of the plant survive).

Hibernate To spend the winter in an inactive, dormant state.

Incomplete metamorphosis In insects, to pass through three distinct physical stages: egg, nymph, adult. Occurs in dragonflies, grasshoppers and others.

Insect An invertebrate animal with six legs and three clearly defined body sections.

Invertebrate Any animal that lacks a spinal cord. Includes insects, molluscs, spiders and many others.

Larva The second stage of an insect that undergoes complete metamorphosis – the larva hatches from the egg and feeds until it is ready to pupate.

Lobe Of leaves, a division in the leaf shape.

Looper A moth caterpillar that moves by strongly arching its body. Often camouflaged to resemble a twig.

Mandibles The jaws of an insect; the upper and lower parts of the bill in birds.

Metamorphosis To transform through distinctly different physical forms on the way to adulthood, as happens with insects and amphibians. *See also* 'Complete metamorphosis' and 'Incomplete metamorphosis'.

Molluscs The animal group containing snails and slugs.

Mouthparts Feeding structures in insects and other invertebrates. They vary in form and function, and may be used to tear, suck, grind or rasp.

Muzzle The projecting snout of a mammal, comprising nose and mouth.

Mycelia The growing, root-like parts of a fungus, normally out of sight underground or within decaying wood.

Naturalised A species that is not native to a certain area, but has become established there following deliberate introduction or accidental release from captivity/spread from cultivation.

Nymph The second stage of an insect that undergoes incomplete metamorphosis – the nymph hatches from the egg, feeds and grows, and then undergoes its final moult to become an adult.

Ovary The female part of a flower, which matures into the fruit after pollination.

Ovipositor Egg-laying organ in some female insects.

Palmate Of leaves, comprising multiple leaflets arranged in a radiating 'hand' shape.

Palps Structures on head of butterfly or moth, which protect the proboscis when not in use.

Parasite A species that habitually exploits another, sometimes by literally living on or inside it.

Parotoid gland A large skin gland found behind the eye in some amphibians. It secretes a noxious-tasting substance to deter predators.

Parthenogenesis To reproduce by cloning, without mating taking place.

Pedipalps Short, leg-like structures on a spider's head, used in feeding.

Perennial A plant that lives for an indefinite number of years, in some cases dying back in winter but regenerating again in spring.

Pinnate Of leaves, comprising multiple leaflets that grow along a leaf stem in opposite or alternate pairs.

Pollination Fertilisation of plants by applying pollen (male sex cells) to the stigma, from where it reaches the ovary to fertilise the eggs inside.

Proboscis Tubular mouthpart of an insect, used to suck nectar from flowers or sap from plant stems.

Prostrate Of plant stems, growing flat along the ground.

Pupa The third stage of an insect that undergoes complete metamorphosis – the mature larva pupates, and the adult develops in, and emerges from, the pupa.

Scalloping Of animal patterning, describes C-shaped markings, such as light fringes on otherwise dark, rounded feathers.

Sepal Green leaf-like structures that cover a growing flower bud, and may support the corolla when the flower is open.

Spore The 'seed' of a fungus or moss; very fine reproductive grains produced by mushrooms.

Stamen The male part of a plant, which produces pollen.

Stigma An extension of a plant ovary, which receives pollen.

Streaking Of animal patterning, describes fine stripes that run along the body rather than across it.

Territorial Of animals, inclined to establish a home range and drive others (usually of the same sex and species) away from it.

Thorax The middle of the three body segments of an insect, to which the wings and legs are attached.

Tragus Pointed projection inside a mammal's ear, very obvious in bats.

Venation Of plant parts or insect wings, describes the pattern of the veins.

Venomous Of animals, able to inject toxins into another animal's body via a bite.

Woody plant A plant with woody stems that do not die back at the end of the growing season. Includes trees and shrubs.

Female

Sparrowhawk ■ *Accipiter nisus*
male 32cm; female 38cm (length)

DESCRIPTION Long-tailed raptor with rounded wings, yellow or reddish eyes, and long yellow legs. Male has grey-blue upperparts, with dark bands on tail and sometimes some round white patches on back; pale below with reddish-orange barring. Under-tail area white. Female browner above with white eyebrows, and white below with dark barring. Young birds browner with coarser barring.
DISTRIBUTION Common resident across Europe; summer visitor in N Scandinavia.
HABITS AND HABITAT Hunts small birds (female can take prey up to size of a Woodpigeon). Uses hedges as cover to launch surprise attacks. Soars high on fine days, in characteristic flap-flap-glide flight. Bathes frequently. Builds a stick nest in trees, and has 1 brood per year of 4–6 chicks. Usually silent, but may call *kewkewkewkew*. Gardens, parks and woodland.

Feral Pigeon ■ *Columba livia* 33cm (length)

DESCRIPTION Sturdy pigeon with red legs, dark bill and white waxy cere. Descended from domestic pigeons; plumage varies greatly. 'Wild-type' has light grey wings with double black bar, white rump. Most others are various shades of grey, some pure white, pure black or red-brown. Usually has purple-green gloss on neck; eyes orange-red. Underwings always white. Young birds have duller eyes and plumage, and smoother and duller cere.
DISTRIBUTION Common in towns across Europe; resident.
HABITS AND HABITAT Gregarious, nesting and foraging in groups. Feeds on the ground,

eating seeds and discarded scraps. Its flight is fast and strong. Nests on buildings, laying 2 eggs in an untidy nest. May breed at any time of year. Calls are various coos. Male courtship involves strutting and loud cooing. Commonest in larger towns and cities.

Woodpigeon
■ *Columba palumbus* 40cm (length)

DESCRIPTION Large, plump, short-legged pigeon. Pale ash-grey, with white patch on neck and white along bottom edge of wing (crescent-shaped in flight); pinkish flush on breast, green-purple iridescence on neck, and dark flight feathers and tail band. Legs red, bill orange-pink, cere white, eyes pale. Juveniles lack the white neck-patch, and have dark eyes and duller bill.
DISTRIBUTION Common across Europe; summer visitor in N Scandinavia, otherwise resident.
HABITS AND HABITAT Eats seeds, tree buds and other plant matter. Has a waddling gait. Forms large flocks in winter. Builds a stick nest in trees, laying 1–2 eggs, usually in midsummer. Call is a soft, soothing *oo-rooo-coo*; song is a 5-syllable coo. Claps wings in display flight. Found wherever there are trees.

Collared Dove
■ *Streptopelia decaocto* 32cm (length)

DESCRIPTION Dainty, long-tailed dove. Neat, narrow black band around nape, bordered with white (absent in juvenile). Plumage otherwise pale sandy grey-brown, darker on wings. Bottom edge of wing paler grey, forming a broad, light band across wing in flight. Flight feathers darker grey. Tail has white corners on upperside, white on underside with blackish base. Dark eyes and bill, small greyish cere, red legs.
DISTRIBUTION Common resident across Europe.
HABITS AND HABITAT Usually seen alone or in pairs, sometimes in small groups in winter. Feeds mainly on the ground, eating seeds and other plant matter. Spread rapidly westwards from Asia in the 20th century. Nests in trees, laying 2 eggs in a flimsy stick nest. Call is an emphatic *krooo*; song is *coo OO cuk*. Has a steeply rising and falling display flight. Common on farmland and anywhere there are trees.

Tawny Owl
■ *Strix aluco* 38cm (length)

DESCRIPTION Large, stocky, big-headed owl. Plumage brown above, with black and cream streaks and bars. Underparts lighter brown with dark streaks. Has large, warm brown facial disc, edged narrowly with black. Eyes black, bill pale. Legs and feet fully feathered. Wings broad, rounded. Newly fledged chicks are covered in faintly barred grey fluff.
DISTRIBUTION Common resident across Europe as far N as central Sweden.
HABITS AND HABITAT Nocturnal. Preys mainly on small mammals, also sometimes on birds and insects. Roosts in trees; pellets of coughed-up bones and fur are found below roost sites. Nests in large tree-holes. Young birds leave the nest before they can fly and climb in branches. Calls are a low, hooting *whoo hooo hoo* (usually given by male) and a sharp, yapping *ke-vick* (mainly female). Woodland.

Swift ■ *Apus apus* 18cm (length)

DESCRIPTION Streamlined bird, almost invariably seen on the wing. Plumage blackish with off-white throat-patch. Wings very long, narrow and sickle-shaped, with bend very close to the body. Tail shortish and clearly forked. Head and body form a cigar shape. Bill very small but gape very wide. Throat sometimes bulges with collected insects. Feet tiny; birds can only cling, not perch.
DISTRIBUTION Summer visitor found across Europe late Apr–Aug.
HABITS AND HABITAT Catches large quantities of small flying insects on the wing, hunting both close to the ground and very high. Alternately glides and rapidly flickers its wings. Gregarious. Nests in cavities in buildings, laying 2–3 eggs. Voice is a loud, shrill, harsh scream; groups often scream in tandem. Travels widely to find good foraging conditions. Breeds in towns and villages.

Green Woodpecker
■ *Picus viridis* 33cm (length)

DESCRIPTION Large, long-billed woodpecker.
Mossy green above and pale grey-green below.
Tail and outer flight feathers dark with narrow
white bars. Rump bright golden green, obvious in
flight. Has bright red crown and black eye-mask,
this extending below eye in a line (solid black in
female, red-centred in male). Eyes pale, legs and
bill grey. Juvenile lacks eye-mask, and is speckled
with white above and black below.
DISTRIBUTION Common resident across Europe
as far N as central Sweden.
HABITS AND HABITAT Pecks at rotten wood to
extract grubs; also eats ants on the ground. Flight
undulating. Nests in holes it excavates in tree
trunks, and lays 5–6 eggs. Call is a series of loud
laughing notes; it 'sings' by drumming rapidly
on resonant branches. Found in woods and open
country.

Female

Great Spotted Woodpecker
■ *Dendrocopos major* 25cm (length)

DESCRIPTION Medium-sized black, white and
red woodpecker. Crown, back, wings and tail
black; face, shoulder-patch and underparts white.
Also has a black stripe from bill base to nape, and
another from shoulder curving down onto breast;
the stripes cross to leave a small white neck-
patch. Forehead patch off-white, flight and tail
feathers narrowly barred white. Under-tail bright
red; male also has red patch on back of neck.
Juvenile has all-red crown and pinkish under-tail.
DISTRIBUTION Common resident across
Europe; absent from Ireland.
HABITS AND HABITAT Feeds on trees,
extracting grubs from rotten wood. Sometimes
takes young birds. Also often visits garden
birdfeeders. Flight undulating. Excavates a nest-
hole in a trunk or branch, and lays 5–6 eggs.
Call is a sharp *kick*; 'song' is a rapid drumming.
Woodlands and parks.

Female

Swallow
▪ *Hirundo rustica* 19cm (length)

DESCRIPTION Small, long-tailed bird, usually seen on the wing. Upperparts, face and breast blackish with a strong violet-blue sheen. Has a small, dark orange forehead-patch and large throat-patch. Underparts off-white. Tail forked, with very long outer feathers ('streamers'). From below, flight feathers appear dark, rest of underwing pale, white spots on tail feathers. Eyes dark, as are the tiny bill, short legs and feet. Juvenile has a shorter tail and duller plumage.
DISTRIBUTION Common summer visitor across Europe.
HABITS AND HABITAT Catches small flying insects, often hunting very close to the ground. Also often feeds over water. Flight fast and agile. Gregarious, especially on migration. Nests in outbuildings or caves, attaching a mud nest to a vertical surface. Has 2 or 3 broods of 3–6. Call is a sharp *tswit*; song is a pleasant trilling twitter. Most often seen in low-lying, open countryside.

House Martin ▪ *Delichon urbicum* 13cm (length)

DESCRIPTION Similar to Swallow (*above*) in size, shape and general character, but lacks long tail streamers. Upperparts black with subtle blue gloss. Has large white rump-patch. Crown and upper face black, chin, breast and belly white. Legs and feet fully feathered white. Underwings greyish, flight feathers darker than inner feathers. Eyes and bill dark. Tail forked. Juvenile slightly dusky below.
DISTRIBUTION Common summer visitor throughout Europe.
HABITS AND HABITAT Feeding behaviour similar to that of Swallow. Builds a mud cup

nest under eaves of buildings, often close to others; flocks collect mud from puddles in spring. Has 2 or 3 broods of 3–5. Call is a dry *trrrt*; song is a soft twitter. Found in all open countryside; will use more urban environments than Swallows.

Pied Wagtail
■ *Motacilla alba yarelli* 18cm (length)

DESCRIPTION Small, long-tailed, lively bird. Male Pied has white face and belly; black crown, throat, breast and back. Wings black with white bars, tail black with white outer feathers. Bill, legs and eyes dark. Females duskier and greyer. Winter adult has white chin. Juveniles have black breast-patch only, otherwise grey and yellow-white. **White Wagtail** *M. a. alba*, found on the Continent, is very similar but males have a grey back.

DISTRIBUTION Common resident in W and S Europe; summer visitor E of Belgium. Pied Wagtail occurs in Britain and Ireland, White Wagtail elsewhere in Europe.

HABITS AND HABITAT Insect-eater, feeding mainly on the ground; also flycatches. Runs rapidly; when still, constantly bobs tail. Nests in cavities in walls, buildings or similar, having 1 or 2 broods of 3–8. Call is a bright *chissik*; song is a subdued twitter. Found in towns and open countryside, often by water.

TOP: *Pied Wagtail*; ABOVE: *White Wagtail*

Waxwing
■ *Bombycilla garrulus* 18cm (length)

DESCRIPTION Very distinctive chunky, smallish bird with a long crest. Plumage soft orange-brown, with a paler belly and grey rump; black chin, eye-stripe and flight feathers; 2 short white bands in wings; red tips to secondary feathers and yellow tips to primaries; broad yellow band at tail-tip. Eyes dark; legs and short, stoutish bill dark grey.

LEFT: *male*
ABOVE: *female*

DISTRIBUTION Winter visitor to N Europe, its abundance varying greatly from year to year. Breeds in N Sweden and further N and E.

HABITS AND HABITAT In most of our region it visits in flocks (sometimes very large) and searches for berry-bearing trees, which are soon stripped of their fruit. Acrobatic and very approachable when feeding. Call is a high, ringing *sirrrr*. Breeds in remote coniferous forest, but winter birds often visit parks and gardens.

Wren ■ *Troglodytes troglodytes* 10cm (length)

DESCRIPTION Very small, short-tailed bird.
Wings very short and tail often held cocked
above back. Upperparts warm reddish brown,
underparts lighter grey-brown, with fine, darker
barring all over, most noticeably on wings and
tail. Has a dark eye-stripe and pale eyebrow.
Bill dark, slender and slightly downcurved.
Eyes dark, legs pinkish.
DISTRIBUTION Common resident across most
of Europe; summer visitor to N Scandinavia.
HABITS AND HABITAT Feeds mainly on the
ground or in low vegetation, taking insects,
spiders and other small invertebrates. Quite
shy and skulking. Male builds multiple basic
nests, then female chooses 1 and completes
construction. Has 1 or 2 broods of 5–8.
Call is a hard, rattling *tic tic tic*; song is a
loud, powerful trill with rapid 'machine-gun'
rattles. Found wherever there is low cover.

Dunnock
■ *Prunella modularis* 14cm (length)

DESCRIPTION Unobtrusive sparrow-sized bird.
Blue-grey head and breast, with brown cheeks
and crown. Belly whitish; plumage otherwise
mostly warm brown, with dark streaks on back
and flanks, but no really striking markings.
Eyes dark red-brown, slender bill dark, legs pink.
Juvenile is more heavily streaked, with less grey.
DISTRIBUTION Common resident across most
of W Europe, including extreme S of Sweden;
summer visitor further N.
HABITS AND HABITAT Shy and quiet. Feeds
mainly on the ground, taking insects and other
invertebrates, as well as seeds and berries. Often
flicks its wings. Has a complex breeding system;
both sexes may have multiple mates. Females
have up to 3 broods of 4–6 a year. Call is a
shrill *tsweep*; song (given from high perch)
is a high-pitched warble. Found in most
wooded or scrubby habitats.

Robin

▪ *Erithacus rubecula* 14cm (length)

DESCRIPTION Perky, sparrow-sized bird. Red face and breast with a soft greyish border, upperparts otherwise plain warm brown and underparts whitish with brown wash on flanks. Large, dark eyes; slender, dark bill; longish, dark brown legs. Juvenile warm brown, with pale speckles over back, head and underparts; belly whitish; vague, pale wing bar. DISTRIBUTION Common resident across most of W Europe, including extreme S of Sweden; summer visitor further N. HABITS AND HABITAT Eats invertebrates, also seeds and berries. Feeds mainly on the ground; hops rapidly.

Garden birds sometimes become very tame. Nests in natural or man-made crevices; has 2 or 3 broods of 4–6. Extremely territorial. Calls are a *tic* and *tsweee*; song is a high, descending, sweet, melancholic warble. Woods, hedges and other well-vegetated habitats.

Black Redstart

▪ *Phoenicurus ochruros* 14cm (length)

DESCRIPTION Similar to Robin (*above*) in size and shape. Male smoky black, paler on crown and back, with white patch on secondaries; paler belly. Rump red, tail red with dark centre. Bill dark, slender; eyes dark; legs blackish. Female and juvenile also have red rump and tail, otherwise dull grey-brown with whitish belly. DISTRIBUTION Resident in SW Europe; summer visitor further N and E. Local and restricted to S in UK and Sweden. HABITS AND HABITAT Constantly quivers its tail, and runs rather than hops (cf. Robin). Insect-eater, feeding on the ground or rooftops; also flycatches.

Usually nests in a crevice in a wall or roof; has 2 or 3 broods of 4–6. Call is a hard, clicking *tac*; song incorporates high twitters interspersed with gravelly noises. Urban environments, but also sea cliffs and other rocky habitats.

Blackbird

■ *Turdus merula* 25cm (length)

DESCRIPTION Medium-sized, well-proportioned, quite long-tailed, dark bird. Male plumage all velvety black, bill and eye-ring yellow (darker in young males), legs dark. Female dark brown with faint darker mottling, no yellow eye-ring and bill darker. Juvenile usually lighter brown than adult female, and with stronger speckling. DISTRIBUTION Common resident across most of Europe; summer visitor to N Scandinavia. HABITS AND HABITAT Moves with bounding hops. Usually flicks its tail upwards when landing. Often forages on lawns, pausing to listen for worms. Eats invertebrates; also berries and other fruit. Builds a cup nest in a bush, rearing 2 or 3 broods of 3–5. Call is a clucking *quick* or *chink*; song (from a high, prominent perch) is a beautiful mellow, fluty warbling. Parkland, woods and towns, including cities.

TOP: *male*; ABOVE: *female*

Fieldfare ■ *Turdus pilaris* 25cm (length)

DESCRIPTION Same size as Blackbird (*above*) but quite colourful. Head and rump blue-grey, back and wings reddish brown, tail and flight feathers blackish. Underparts creamy with orange flush on breast, heavily marked with black crescents; blackish in front of eye and under cheeks; faint white eyebrow. Bill yellow with black tip, eyes and legs dark. In flight, shows white underwings. DISTRIBUTION Resident in much of NE Europe; winter visitor in varying numbers to S and W parts (including UK), summer visitor to N and central Sweden. HABITS AND HABITAT Feeds on invertebrates, berries and fruit. Builds a cup nest in bushes, having 2 broods of 3–5. Call is a soft, chuckling *chuck-check*; song is a rather weak warble. Breeds in woodland and parkland. Very gregarious in winter, often flocking with other thrushes, and feeding on berry bushes in early winter and ploughed fields later on.

Redwing ■ *Turdus iliacus* 21cm (length)

DESCRIPTION Smaller and relatively shorter-tailed than other thrushes. Warm brown above and creamy white below. Dark eye-stripe and prominent creamy eyebrow give it a frowning expression. Dark stripe down chin, leading to dark, streaky spots on breast and fainter spots onto belly. Flanks and underwings brick-red. Bill yellow with dark tip, eyes dark, legs pinkish. Young birds similar, but with softer markings and pale feather edges in wings. DISTRIBUTION Common summer visitor in NW Europe; winter visitor to S and W, including UK. HABITS AND HABITAT Feeding habits similar to those of Fieldfare (p. 24). Nests in coniferous woodland, building a cup nest and rearing 2 broods of 3–6 a year. Call is a thin, harsh *sreeee*, often heard at night from migrating birds; song is a variable, jumbled warble. Winter habits similar to those of Fieldfare.

Song Thrush
■ *Turdus philomelos* 23cm (length)

DESCRIPTION Medium-sized thrush. Warm brown above and creamy white below; underparts marked from breast to belly with neat, teardrop-shaped, dark spots. Face markings subtle, creating a gentle expression. Faint, pale wing bar. In flight, shows yellowish-orange underwings. Eyes dark, bill mid-brown with darker tip, legs dull pink. Juvenile has pale streaks on back. DISTRIBUTION Common resident in NW Europe; summer visitor to Scandinavia. HABITS AND HABITAT Fairly shy thrush, usually not gregarious. Forages mainly on the ground. Has a typical thrush diet, and expertly cracks snails open on favourite stones ('thrushes' anvils'). Builds a cup nest in a bush, rearing 2 or 3 broods of 3–6 a year. Call is a soft *tsick*; song is fluty, with each short phrase repeated 2 or more times. Found wherever there are trees and bushes.

Mistle Thrush
■ *Turdus viscivorus* 27cm (length)

DESCRIPTION Similar but larger and paler than Song Thrush (p. 25). Sandy grey-brown above and whitish below, breast and belly marked with round, dark spots. Has scaly feather fringes at bend of wing. In flight, shows white underwings and tail corners. Eyes dark, bill pinkish with dark tip, legs dull pinkish. Juvenile has scaly appearance to head, pale streaks on back, and dark marking on cheek.

DISTRIBUTION Common resident in NW Europe; summer visitor to Scandinavia.

HABITS AND HABITAT Bolder and more gregarious than Song Thrush. Feeds on invertebrates and fruit. Nesting begins in early spring, with often 2 broods of 3–5 reared in a well-concealed cup nest. Call is a hard, dry rattle; song (from a high perch) is a powerful, rich, fluty but rather monotonous warbling. Found in most habitats where there are tall trees.

Blackcap ■ *Sylvia atricapilla* 13cm (length)

DESCRIPTION Small, slim and quite long-tailed bird. Plumage greyish, lighter below. Male has a neat black cap, not extending to nape. Grey cheeks and whitish chin distinguish it from black-capped tit species. Eyes dark with faint, pale half-ring below; fine bill grey with dark tip; legs mid-grey. Female and juvenile have a rufous-chestnut cap.

DISTRIBUTION Common summer visitor across NW Europe, increasingly present in winter in S UK.

HABITS AND HABITAT Feeds on insects; forages discreetly, mainly in trees and bushes. Eats many berries prior to its migration. In the UK, wintering birds often visit garden

birdfeeders. Nests low in a bush, female choosing from several rudimentary nests built by male. Usually rears 1 brood of 4–6. Call is a hard *tac*; song is a rich, hurried, fluty warble. Woodlands and other habitats with trees.

FAR LEFT: *male*
LEFT: *female*

Chiffchaff

■ *Phylloscopus collybita* 11cm (length)

DESCRIPTION Small, very active bird, similar to Willow Warbler (*below*). Greenish above, darkest on flight feathers and tail, and yellowish below. Dark eye-stripe, yellowish eyebrow and narrow, pale half-ring below eye. Birds from N of region are often paler. Eyes and legs dark, bill darkish.

DISTRIBUTION Common summer visitor across NW Europe, increasingly present in winter in S UK.

HABITS AND HABITAT Restless, often flicking its wings and dipping its tail. Picks insects and other invertebrates from twigs of trees and shrubs; also flycatches. Nests in dense cover close to the ground, rearing 4–7 chicks in a domed nest. Call is a rising *hweet*; song is a steady 2-note *chiff chaff chiff chaff*. Found wherever there are trees; wintering UK birds usually occur in low-lying places, often close to the coast.

Willow Warbler

■ *Phylloscopus trochilus* 11cm (length)

DESCRIPTION Very like a Chiffchaff (*above*), but is slightly brighter with a stronger face pattern (though has a less obvious pale half eye-ring), longer wings and, usually, pale legs. Juvenile is much more strongly washed with yellow on underparts. In general, differences between the call and song of the two species are more reliable identification guides.

DISTRIBUTION Common summer visitor across N and W Europe.

HABITS AND HABITAT Diet and foraging style similar to those of Chiffchaff. Moves around with similar restlessness, though lacks the tail-pumping habit and flicks its wings less often. Builds a well-concealed domed nest on or near the ground; has 1 brood of 4–8, although some males have a 2nd brood with another mate. Call is a disyllabic, upslurred *hooweet*; song is a sweet, steady, descending warble, like Chaffinch's (p. 36) but slower and lacking final flourish. Woodland and scrubland; less often in gardens than Chiffchaff.

Goldcrest
■ *Regulus regulus* 9cm (length)

DESCRIPTION Smallest bird in Europe, 'neckless' and short-tailed. Grey-green above and whitish below, wings darker with double white bar. Crown yellow (with orange centre in male), bordered with black; short, narrow black line from bill base downwards, face otherwise plain with prominent dark eye; small, fine bill dark; legs brownish.
DISTRIBUTION Common resident in NW Europe; summer visitor to N Sweden.
HABITS AND HABITAT Feeds restlessly, mainly in pine trees, picking tiny invertebrates from between needles.
Also flycatches. Often approachable. Builds a deep cup nest suspended from conifer twigs; has 1 or 2 broods of 8–11. Call is a very high, thin *tsee*; song is an equally high, short twitter *di-da-dee, di-da-dee, dididi*. Found anywhere that has even a few conifers.

Spotted Flycatcher
■ *Muscicapa striata* 14.5cm (length)

DESCRIPTION Small, large-headed bird with a very upright stance. Dull grey-brown above with pale fringes to wing feathers, darker flight and tail feathers, and fine, dark streaks on crown; whitish below with faint, darker breast streaks. Eye dark with vague, pale eye-ring. Juvenile has pale speckling above and dark scaling below. Bill dark, fine but broad-based. Legs dark.
DISTRIBUTION Common but declining summer visitor across Europe.
HABITS AND HABITAT Hunts flying insects, dashing out and returning to same perch. Nests in natural or man-made hollows (will use open nestboxes); 1st brood of 4–6, sometimes
a 2nd smaller brood. Call is a squeaky *tzee* or sharp *eez-tchick*; song is quiet, simple and steady, with scratchy and twittered notes. Woodland and parkland with mature trees.

Blue Tit

■ *Cyanistes caeruleus* 11cm (length)

DESCRIPTION Very small, restless and acrobatic. Blue crown; dark eye-stripe, nape and chin; white eyebrows and cheeks. Underparts yellow with a narrow, dark line down belly. Wings blue-green with a white bar; back and tail also blue-green. Juveniles are duller, with yellow cheeks.
DISTRIBUTION Widespread and common resident across Europe.
HABITS AND HABITAT Forages in treetops for invertebrates; also eats seeds and frequently visits garden birdfeeders. Nests in tree-holes and uses nestboxes. Has 1 brood (of sometimes 10 or more chicks) a year. Flocks with other tit

species in winter. Call is a thin *see see see*, alarm call a *churrr-ik-ik*; song is an explosive *ping-ping-ping-churrrrr*. Common wherever there are trees, including city parks and gardens.

Great Tit

■ *Parus major* 14cm (length)

DESCRIPTION Largest tit species across most of the region. Head black with white cheeks. Underparts yellow with black stripe from chin down centre (broader in male). Back mossy green, wings blue-green with single white bar, tail blue-green. Eyes and bill dark, legs greyish. Juvenile duller and paler, with yellow cheeks, pale nape-patch and narrow stripe down breast, this not reaching belly.
DISTRIBUTION Common resident across Europe.
HABITS AND HABITAT Similar to Blue Tit (*above*). Dominates other tit

species at birdfeeders. Nests in tree-holes and natural or artificial cavities, including nestboxes; has 1 brood of 5–12. Calls are very varied but usually short, clear or churring; song comprises 2 repeated notes, *tea-cher tea-cher tea-cher*, more rapid than that of Chiffchaff (p. 27). Woods, parks and gardens, including those in cities.

Marsh Tit
■ *Poecile palustris* 11cm (length)

DESCRIPTION Sleek and agile, the size of a Blue Tit (p. 29). Cap black (extending onto nape), small black bib. Cheeks white, shading abruptly to light brown; underparts whitish with light brown wash on flanks. Upperparts plain grey-brown. Eyes and short bill black, legs dark grey. The very similar **Willow Tit** P. montanus is a less frequent garden visitor; it has whiter cheeks, a fluffier appearance and a different call – a down-slurred, nasal *djeer*.

DISTRIBUTION Fairly common (though declining in places) resident across most of Europe; absent from Scotland, Ireland and N Sweden.

HABITS AND HABITAT Feeds on invertebrates, nuts and seeds. A shy, furtive visitor to birdfeeders. Nests in tree-holes (and nestboxes), producing 1 or 2 broods of 7–9. Call is a sneezing *pitchou*; song is an accelerating trill. Woodland; despite its name, has no particular tie to marshy areas. Flocks with other tits in winter.

Coal Tit
■ *Periparus ater* 11cm (length)

DESCRIPTION Small with a large head. Black cap (reaching nape) and large black bib, large white patch on nape. Upperparts dull blue-grey with double white wing bar, underparts whitish with peachy wash on flanks. Eyes and relatively long bill dark, legs dark grey. Juvenile has yellowish breast and cheeks, and duller black cap.

DISTRIBUTION Common resident across most of Europe.

HABITS AND HABITAT Feeds mainly on insects high in treetops, especially conifers; also takes seeds. A shy visitor to birdfeeders, much bullied by other tits. Will take and hide food to consume later. Nests in tree-holes (and nestboxes), rearing 1 brood of 8–12. Calls and song are similar to, but higher-pitched than, those of Great Tit (p. 29). Woodlands, especially coniferous; also parkland. Less common in cities than Blue Tit (p. 29) and Great Tit.

Long-tailed Tit
■ *Aegithalos caudatus* 14cm (length)

DESCRIPTION Tiny, rotund, very long-tailed bird. Head whitish with a broad blackish stripe above eye reaching back; underparts whitish with dull pink on flanks and under-tail; upperparts black with reddish-pink shoulders, white feather edges on flight feathers and outer tail. Eyes dark with red eye-ring; legs and tiny bill dark. N European birds are paler, with pure white head. Juveniles have shorter tails and a blackish face-mask.
DISTRIBUTION Common resident across most of Europe; patchier distribution in N Sweden.
HABITS AND HABITAT Usually seen in noisy family parties, moving through trees and bushes picking tiny invertebrates from twigs. Builds a beautiful lichen-covered dome nest in deep cover, rearing 1 or 2 broods of 8–12. Calls are a soft *seee* and short *prrrp*. Will flock with other tits. Found in all wooded habitats.

Nuthatch
■ *Sitta europaea* 14cm (length)

DESCRIPTION Stocky, short-tailed and long-billed. Upperparts slate-blue-grey; cheeks white; underparts whitish with red-orange flush, deepening towards white-spotted under-tail. Long, dark eye-stripe. Dagger-like bill dark blue-grey; eyes dark; short, strong legs pinkish orange. N birds much paler, with red restricted to under-tail.
DISTRIBUTION Common resident across much of Europe, becoming patchy into Scotland and N Sweden. Absent from Ireland.
HABITS AND HABITAT Agile tree-climber, which unlike woodpeckers does not use its tail for support and can descend head-first. Eats insects, seeds and nuts, wedging nuts into bark cracks to hammer them open. Nests in tree-holes, using mud to narrow the entrance hole to preferred size. Rears 1 or 2 broods of 6–8. Call is a ringing *tuit*; song is whistled and variable. Found wherever there are mature trees.

Treecreeper ■ *Certhia familiaris* 12.5cm (length)

DESCRIPTION Small, long-tailed and long-billed bird. Upperparts brown with white streaks on head, yellowish streaks on back; underparts from chin to under-tail white, faint brown wash on under-tail. Broad white eyebrow; broad, zigzag-shaped, dark-edged yellowish wing bar. Bill fine, downcurved, dark brown. Eyes dark, legs pinkish.

DISTRIBUTION Common resident in UK and Europe E of central France; patchier in N Sweden. The very similar Short-toed Treecreeper C. *brachydactyla* occurs in SW Europe.

HABITS AND HABITAT Climbs trees in a spiral from the base, probing bark for invertebrate prey. Moves jerkily, using tail as a prop. Nests in a bark crevice, rearing 1 or 2 broods of 5–6. Call is a very high *tsee*; song is high, soft twitter and warble. Found wherever there are mature trees.

Jay ■ *Garrulus glandarius* 34cm (length)

DESCRIPTION Colourful, relatively small crow. Mainly pinkish brown, with black streaks on white crown; broad black moustache stripe; black-barred, bright blue patch at bend of wing; tail black; rump white; flight feathers black with short white bar on secondaries. Broad-winged, tail

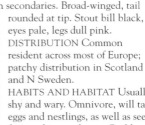

rounded at tip. Stout bill black, eyes pale, legs dull pink.

DISTRIBUTION Common resident across most of Europe; patchy distribution in Scotland and N Sweden.

HABITS AND HABITAT Usually shy and wary. Omnivore, will take eggs and nestlings, as well as seeds, fruit and invertebrates. Builds a twig nest in a tree, rearing 5–7 young. Call is a loud, harsh scream. Collects and buries many acorns in autumn, and is most visible at this time of year flying to and fro in a slow-flapping, ponderous-looking flight. Sometimes somewhat gregarious when not breeding.

Magpie

■ *Pica pica* 45cm (length)

DESCRIPTION Unmistakable long-tailed crow. Plumage mainly black with bluish gloss on wings, greenish on tail. Central breast and belly white; long, narrow white shoulder-patch; primaries white with black edges (look all black on closed wing). Eyes and sturdy bill dark, legs dark grey-pink. Wings short and round, tail graduated and as long as body (shorter in juvenile).
DISTRIBUTION Common resident throughout Europe.
HABITS AND HABITAT Often seen in pairs or small parties. Omnivorous

and opportunistic, bold and alert but often quite approachable. Often searches for food on ground, moving with hops or a strutting swagger. Builds a large roofed twig nest in a tree or big shrub, and has 1 brood of 3–9. Call is a hard, rattling chatter or softer cluck. Found in most environments, including city centre parks.

Jackdaw

■ *Corvus monedula* 37cm (length)

DESCRIPTION The smallest of the black crows. Plumage black all over apart from the nape, which shades into a silvery-grey colour. Looks relatively small-billed and round-headed. Eyes pale (unlike any other black crow), bill and legs dark. Juvenile has uniformly black plumage, eyes darker than adult but still clearly light-coloured.
DISTRIBUTION Common resident throughout Europe.
HABITS AND HABITAT Gregarious,

usually foraging in small or large groups. Often flocks with Rooks (p. 34). Agile and acrobatic in flight, wingbeats faster and deeper than those of larger crows. Omnivorous, mainly searching for food on the ground. Urban birds become very approachable. Nests in rock crannies, tree-holes or buildings (especially chimneys), often in colonies, rearing 1 brood of 4–5. Call is a ringing *tjack*. Open countryside, villages and towns.

LEFT: *Carrion Crow*; RIGHT: *Hooded Crow*

Carrion Crow

▪ *Corvus corone*
48cm (length)

DESCRIPTION
Large, sturdy crow with all-black plumage. Eyes, heavy bill and strong, thick legs black. **Hooded Crow** *C. cornix*, alike except in plumage, is sometimes considered a subspecies of Carrion Crow; it has a mid-grey body with black wings, tail, head and upper breast. Where both coexist, hybridisation occurs, producing birds with variable amounts of grey.

DISTRIBUTION Carrion Crow occurs in W Europe, and is replaced by Hooded E of Germany; Hooded also replaces Carrion in Ireland and NW Scotland.

HABITS AND HABITAT Often solitary but may gather in groups, especially in cities. Omnivore; opportunistic feeder, foraging mainly on the ground. Builds a large stick nest in a tree, rearing 1 brood of 2–7. Call is the familiar hard cawing *kraaa*. Found in all kinds of habitats, including coastal and urban environments.

Rook ▪ *Corvus frugilegus* 46cm (length)

DESCRIPTION Slightly smaller than Carrion Crow (*above*). Plumage all black, looser and shaggier than that of Carrion Crow. Patch of bare white skin around bill base; rather peaked crown. Bill slightly more pointed than Carrion Crow's, white at base shading to dark grey; eyes and legs dark. Juvenile lacks bare skin, so very similar to Carrion Crow – to separate it, look for peaked crown and looser plumage, especially around legs ('baggy trousers').

DISTRIBUTION Common resident in W and central Europe; patchier in Scandinavia and absent from central Sweden northwards.

HABITS AND HABITAT Gregarious, nesting colonially and foraging in groups. More vegetarian than Carrion Crow. Large rookeries may contain hundreds of stick nests in several adjacent trees, each pair rearing a brood of 2–5. Calls are grating caws. Rural open habitats with trees; often feeds on farmland.

Starling

■ *Sturnus vulgaris* 21cm (length)

DESCRIPTION Stocky, short-tailed and upright smallish bird. Plumage black with strong green and violet gloss. Eyes dark, bill yellow (flushed blue in male) and legs pink. Winter adult has pale brown spots all over; bill and legs duller, darker. Juvenile pale dull grey-brown, developing pale-spotted black winter plumage on underparts first. DISTRIBUTION Common resident across most of W and S Europe; summer visitor in Sweden.
HABITS AND HABITAT Gregarious, especially in winter, when huge roosts may form. Feeds mainly on invertebrates on the ground; also opportunistically takes plant

matter and scraps. Nests in hollows in trees or buildings, rearing 1 or 2 broods of 4–6. Call is a harsh, downslurred *tsheer*; song is a soft, prolonged jumble of squeaks, rattles and whistles. Mimics other birds and mechanical sounds. All environments, including city centres.

House Sparrow

■ *Passer domesticus* 14cm (length)

DESCRIPTION Small, thick-billed bird. Male has a grey crown and rump, black patch in front of eye and large black bib (smaller in winter); side of crown, neck, back, wings and tail brown; underparts pale grey. Female and juvenile greyish below and grey-brownish above, with pale eyebrow. Both sexes have streaked backs and a white wing bar (brighter in male). Eyes dark, bill blackish (male) or grey-brown (female); legs dull grey-pink. DISTRIBUTION Common resident throughout Europe.
HABITS AND HABITAT Gregarious, nesting in loose colonies and feeding in flocks. Eats seeds and insects, also discarded scraps in cities. Usually nests in hollows, including old nests of House Martins (p. 20). Has 2 or 3 broods of 3–5. Call is a loud chirp; song comprises repeated chirps. Found in urban environments (declining in many European cities) and open countryside.

Tree Sparrow
■ *Passer montanus* 13cm (length)

DESCRIPTION Similar to male House Sparrow (p. 35), but has chestnut-brown rather than grey crown and rump, underparts pale brownish rather than greyish, much smaller black bib and distinctive neat black spot on white cheeks. Sexes alike. Juvenile has slightly duller and more diffuse face pattern.

DISTRIBUTION Common resident across much of Europe. Occurs patchily in Ireland, Great Britain and central Sweden; absent from N Sweden.

HABITS AND HABITAT Similar to House Sparrow. Nests in hollows (readily uses nestboxes) and rears 2 or 3 broods of 3–7 a year. Call and song are higher-pitched and have more metallic chirps than those of House Sparrow. More restricted to rural habitats than House Sparrow. Will flock with House Sparrows and farmland finches and buntings.

Chaffinch ■ *Fringilla coelebs* 14cm (length)

DESCRIPTION Slim, perky finch, the size of a House Sparrow (p. 35). Male colourful: small black forehead-patch, blue-grey crown and neck, pink face and underparts, red-brown back, and black wings with double white wing bar. Bill greyish or brownish, eyes dark, legs dull pink. Female and juvenile have double white wing bar, otherwise mid-brown with green tinge, darker above, and with faint pale eyebrow.

DISTRIBUTION Common resident across most of Europe; summer visitor to Sweden.

HABITS AND HABITAT Feeds on seeds and insects, mainly on the ground, and often visits birdfeeders. Builds a delicate cup nest in a tree or bush; has 1 or 2 broods of 3–4. Call is a bright, loud *pink*; song is a descending chatter ending in a flourish. Gregarious in winter, and will flock with other small seed-eaters. Found in most habitats, including cities.

TOP LEFT: *male*
LEFT: *female*

Brambling
■ *Fringilla montifringilla* 14cm (length)

DESCRIPTION Similar in size and shape to Chaffinch (p. 36). Breeding male has black head, bill, back, wings and tail; orange and white wing bars; orange shoulders and breast; white rump and belly, with blackish spots on flanks. Legs dark pinkish orange, eyes dark. Winter male has paler, duller head; bill yellow with dark tip. Female similar, but cheeks light brown and sides of neck grey; dark spots on shoulders.
DISTRIBUTION Summer visitor to central and N Sweden, winter visitor to S and W Europe.
HABITS AND HABITAT Very similar to Chaffinch. Nests in birch forests, with breeding behaviour like that of Chaffinch. Call is an upslurred *tchaaay*; song is a slow, mournful, repeated, buzzing *dzeeee*. Gregarious, winter birds often joining Chaffinch flocks; usually shyer than Chaffinch. Most often seen in farmland with copses and hedgerows.

TOP: *male, winter;* ABOVE: *female*

Greenfinch
■ *Carduelis chloris* 15cm (length)

DESCRIPTION Largish, stocky, large-headed and heavy-billed finch. Male mossy green with a greyish wash on cheeks, flanks and secondaries; primaries and centre of tail dark; bottom edge of wing and sides of tail yellow. Bill light grey-horn, eyes dark, legs dull pink. Female similar but green colour duller and greyer. Juvenile paler with streaks on underparts.
DISTRIBUTION Common resident across most of Europe; summer visitor to central and N Sweden.
HABITS AND HABITAT Feeds mainly on seeds, on the ground and in treetops. Visits birdfeeders, where it dominates tits and other finches. Builds a bulky nest in a tree or shrub, rearing 2 or 3 broods of 4–6. Calls are various high twitters and buzzy, slurred notes; song (from a high perch or circling song-flight) combines several call types. Quite gregarious in winter. Found in most habitats, including city centres.

TOP: *male;* ABOVE: *female*

Goldfinch ■ *Carduelis carduelis* 12cm (length)

DESCRIPTION Smallish, slim finch. Face red with small black eye-mask, cheeks white, crown and sides of neck black. Back and breast warm pinkish brown, rump whitish, wings black with broad yellow bar, tail black, tail- and wing-tips with small white spots. Longish conical bill pale and dark-tipped, eyes dark, legs greyish. Juvenile has adult wing and tail pattern, otherwise pale brown with faint dark streaks.

DISTRIBUTION Common resident across most of Europe; in Sweden summer visitor in S only.

HABITS AND HABITAT Feeds on seeds and insects, favouring thistles and teasels. Attracted to special Nyjer-seed garden birdfeeders. Nest is a neat cup built near a branch tip; has 2 or 3 broods of 4–6 a year. Call is a high, bright tinkling; song is similar but includes trills and wheezes. Gregarious when not breeding.

Siskin ■ *Carduelis spinus* 12cm (length)

DESCRIPTION Small, tit-like finch with notched tail. Male has yellow head and breast with blackish crown, eye-stripe and small bib. Cheeks and back green with fine streaks; wings and central tail blackish; rump, wing bars and sides of tail yellow. Legs and longish conical bill pale greyish, eyes dark. Female duller with plain, streaky green face; rump and wing bars greenish yellow. Juvenile even duller and streakier.

DISTRIBUTION Common resident in most of N Europe; summer visitor in N Sweden, winter visitor to S UK.

HABITS AND HABITAT Feeds on seeds and insects, mainly in treetops. Agile. Visits birdfeeders. Rears 2 broods of 3–5 in a cup nest high in a tree. Call is a clear *tsuuuu*; song is a sweet, wheezy twitter. Very gregarious in winter. Breeds in woodlands; in winter, found wherever there are mature trees.

FAR LEFT: *male*
LEFT: *female*

Bullfinch

■ *Pyrrhula pyrrhula* 14.5cm (length)

DESCRIPTION Largish finch. Male has a black cap and bib; bright pink cheeks and underparts, grey back; white rump and under-tail; black wings with white bar and black tail. Eyes and short, stout bill black; legs greyish. Female similar but dull brownish below rather than pink. Juvenile lacks black on head and is more yellow-brown above and below.
DISTRIBUTION Common resident across N and W Europe.
HABITS AND HABITAT Shy, skulking bird of trees and hedgerows. Eats buds, seeds and insects. Builds a flimsy nest in

ABOVE: *male*; RIGHT: *female*

a thick bush, rearing 1–3 broods of 3–6 a year. Call is a brief, soft whistle; song is a quiet, tentative warble. Usually seen in pairs or sometimes small groups, and does not stray far from cover. Rural habitats with plenty of bushes.

Lesser Redpoll ■ *Carduelis cabaret* 11–12cm (length)

DESCRIPTION Small, agile finch. Plumage brown above and pale below, with dark streaks all over. Black stripe between eye and bill, small black bib. Breeding male has red forehead-patch and pink-flushed breast; in non-breeding male and female these are less red/pink, and in juvenile they are absent. Small bill yellowish, eyes and legs dark. **Common Redpoll** C. *flammea* is sometimes considered a subspecies of Lesser Redpoll; it is very similar but slightly larger and greyer.
DISTRIBUTION Resident in most of UK and parts of N Europe, winter visitor elsewhere.
HABITS AND HABITAT Similar to Siskin (p. 38), feeding in treetops. Nests in tall bush,

having 1 or 2 broods of 4–6 in an untidy cup nest. Call is a metallic trill; song (usually given in song-flight) includes this and twitters. Gregarious, flocks roving in treetops and often joining groups of Siskins. Favours places with alder trees.

LEFT: *Lesser Redpoll*
ABOVE: *Common Redpoll*

Hawfinch

▪ *Coccothraustes coccothraustes* 18cm (length)

DESCRIPTION Large, big-headed and very heavy-billed finch. Plumage soft orange-pink, darker above; black patch between eye, bill and bib; greyish neck; broad white wing bar; flight feathers dark bluish; tail-tip white. Bill grey, eyes mid-brown, legs light pink. Female slightly duller. Juvenile barred below and lacks black face markings.

DISTRIBUTION Patchily distributed resident across most of Europe; absent from Ireland and all but S Sweden.

HABITS AND HABITAT Shy, usually seen in treetops. Feeds mainly on large tree seeds. Builds a shallow, flimsy nest in a tree, and rears 2 or 3 broods of 4–5. Call is a hard, Robin-like *tic*; song is buzzy, slow, simple and quiet. Somewhat gregarious in winter, roosting in groups. Woodlands, especially those with Hornbeam *Carpinus betulus*.

Reed Bunting ▪ *Emberiza schoeniculus* 15cm (length)

DESCRIPTION Sparrow-like bird. Male has a black head and upper breast, with narrow white moustache stripe joining white collar. Back and wings brown, streaked with black; rump grey; tail dark with white edges. Underparts greyish white with dark streaks. Bill blackish, eyes dark, legs dull grey-pink. Female similar but with brown head, light eyebrow and chin.

DISTRIBUTION Common resident in NW Europe; summer visitor in Sweden and parts of Scotland.

HABITS AND HABITAT Rather shy. Closely associated with marshes and wetlands. Eats reed and rush seeds and insects. Nests in a bush, rearing up to 3 broods of 4–5. Call is a shrill *tsiu*; song (from a prominent perch) is a simple, repetitive *twee twee twit-twit-twit*. In winter, may visit farmland and gardens, feeding on the ground with other small seed-eaters.

LEFT: *male*; ABOVE: *female*

Yellowhammer

■ *Emberiza citrinella*
16cm (length)

LEFT: *male*
ABOVE: *female*

DESCRIPTION Largish, long-tailed finch-like bird. Male has a bright yellow head and underparts, with brownish streaks across breast, on flanks and on crown and cheeks; back and wings streaky brown; rump rufous and tail dark. Bill grey, eyes dark, legs dull pinkish. Female duller yellow with heavier markings on head and underparts; juvenile duller still.

DISTRIBUTION Common resident across most of Europe; summer visitor to N Sweden and parts of Scotland.

HABITS AND HABITAT Insect- and seed-eater, feeding in bushes and on the ground. Nests among tall vegetation on the ground, rearing 2 or 3 broods of 3–5. Call is a buzzy *zip*; song is a fast chatter ending with a drawn-out, wheezing note ('a-little-bit-of-bread-and-no cheese'). Often seen in pairs; favours open country with plenty of bushes.

Hedgehog

■ *Erinaceus europaeus* 25cm

DESCRIPTION Stocky, short-legged mammal with a very short tail. Upperside from forehead to tail entirely covered with dull brown spines. Face, legs and underside furry, usually a shade lighter than spines but sometimes almost white, blackish around face and eyes. Muzzle pointed, ears small and round, eyes small and dark. When threatened, curls up to hide vulnerable parts, becoming a ball of spines.

DISTRIBUTION Common across W Europe as far N as central Sweden.

HABITS AND HABITAT Nocturnal. Forages on the ground, snuffling loudly as it does so; omnivorous, but mainly takes slugs, snails, insects and other invertebrates. Does not burrow into the ground but makes a nest in dry leaves for hibernation (Oct–Apr) and breeding. Has 1 or 2 litters of 4–5. Youngsters remain with mother for several weeks. Mainly woodlands.

Mole ▪ *Talpa europaea* 14cm

DESCRIPTION Small, distinctive mammal, adapted for a burrowing lifestyle. Fur black, dense and velvety. Paws and pointed muzzle furless, pink. Front paws large, spade-like, with long, strong claws; back paws much smaller. Tail furred, short and thin. Eyes and ears tiny, barely visible. Above the ground it moves on its belly, sometimes surprisingly quickly.

DISTRIBUTION Found across W Europe as far N as S Sweden. Absent from Ireland.

HABITS AND HABITAT Active day and night, year-round. Rarely seen above ground – mounds of displaced earth on the surface (molehills) reveal its presence. Each individual digs and continually extends its own network of tunnels, eating earthworms and other underground invertebrates as it goes. Males visit females to mate in spring; 1 litter of 2–7 is born in an underground chamber. Found in nearly all habitats.

Pygmy Shrew
▪ *Sorex minutus* 5cm (9cm including tail)

DESCRIPTION Very small, long-tailed and long-muzzled shrew. Fur greyish brown, clearly paler underneath. Tail furred, slender, almost as long as body. Snout long and pointed, with long whiskers. Eyes dark and very small; ears rounded and small, not projecting noticeably from head. Paws lightly furred, legs short.

DISTRIBUTION Common across Europe.

HABITS AND HABITAT Active day and night, year-round. Solitary and fiercely territorial except when breeding. Feeds almost continually when active, eating any invertebrates it can catch – unafraid of people. Makes tunnels or runways though leaf litter or ground vegetation, and will use underground tunnels made by other small mammals. Makes a surface nest; breeds throughout summer, rearing several litters of 5–7. Found in all habitats with ground vegetation.

Common Shrew
■ *Sorex araneus* 7cm (10cm including tail)

DESCRIPTION Very similar to Pygmy
Shrew (p. 42), although normally larger;
best way to separate species is by relative
tail length – in Pygmy, tail is almost as long
as body, whereas in Common it is a little
over half as long. Common also has subtle
reddish stripe on sides, separating grey-
brown upperside from paler underside.
DISTRIBUTION Common across most of
Europe (absent from Ireland). In France
and immediately adjacent areas it is
replaced by the almost identical **Crowned
Shrew** *S. coronatus*.

HABITS AND HABITAT Lifestyle and breeding behaviour very similar to Pygmy Shrew.
Common Shrew may tackle slightly larger prey than Pygmy, including earthworms, which
Pygmies rarely eat. Both species may squeak loudly during territorial disputes. Found in all
vegetated habitats, requiring slightly denser ground cover than Pygmy.

Bank Vole ■ *Clethrionomys glareolus* 9.5cm (14.5cm including tail)

DESCRIPTION Blunt-muzzled, small, stocky mammal, the most mouse-like of voles. Fur
rich reddish brown, greyer on flanks and paler on underside. Eyes rather large, dark. Ears
round and smallish, not projecting noticeably from head. Tail half length of body, furred
and slender. Legs short, paws small.
DISTRIBUTION Common across most of N Europe; recent and spreading colonist in
Ireland; absent from extreme N of Sweden.
HABITS AND HABITAT Active day and night, year-round. Uses underground and surface
tunnels; also climbs in bushes and on fallen trees. Eats plant matter (nuts, seeds and fruit)
and some invertebrates. Produces several litters of 3–5 between spring and autumn in a
nest hidden in surface vegetation or just underground. Found in all habitats with ground
vegetation.

Yellow-necked Mouse
■ *Apodemus flavicollis*
11.5cm (23cm including tail)

DESCRIPTION Small, sleek mammal with a very long tail. Fur warm brown above, white below, with s diamond or triangle of yellowish fur between front paws. Muzzle pointed; eyes large, dark and beady; ears large, petal-shaped, projecting well clear of head. Tail furless and tapering to a point. Legs clearly longer than those of a vole or shrew.
DISTRIBUTION Common in E Europe as far N as central Sweden; patchily distributed in the Netherlands and S UK.
HABITS AND HABITAT Nocturnal. Mainly vegetarian, eating nuts, seeds and fruits, along with the odd invertebrate. Uses tunnels above and below ground but will cross open ground; also jumps high, climbs easily and has been observed in treetops. Often enters houses and other buildings. Has several litters of 4–7 a year in an underground nest. Woodlands.

Wood Mouse
■ *Apodemus sylvaticus*
9.5cm (20cm including tail)

DESCRIPTION Resembles Yellow-necked Mouse (*above*), with beady eyes, prominent ears, a long, furless tail and a pointed muzzle. Distinguished by slightly duller, more yellowy-brown upperside; underside less clean white; and yellow chest spot absent or much reduced.
DISTRIBUTION Common across Europe, as far N as central Sweden. Commoner than Yellow-necked Mouse in most places.
HABITS AND HABITAT Feeding and breeding behaviour very similar to Yellow-necked Mouse, but tends to be seen above ground less often, and is less inclined to enter houses. Will visit bird tables if they are accessible. Neither species hibernates, but they become less active in winter and may gather in communal sleeping areas for warmth; both also store surplus food and may use bird nestboxes for either of these purposes.

House Mouse ■ *Mus domesticus*
8.5cm (17cm including tail)

DESCRIPTION Similar to Wood Mouse (p. 44) but with less prominent eyes and ears. Fur variable, from mid-brown through brown-grey to blackish, paler underneath and with less clean delineation between the colours than in Wood or Yellow-necked (p. 44) Mice. No yellow chest marking. Tail furless and scaly, with clear rings along its length.
DISTRIBUTION Common throughout Europe.
HABITS AND HABITAT Mainly nocturnal. Opportunistic feeder, eating almost anything but favouring plant matter such as nuts and grain. Agile climber and jumper. Vocal, giving loud squeaks. In colonies, males defend small territories, while females may share nests. Breeding takes place year-round, with 4–8 in each litter. Most House Mice live in close proximity to people, and readily establish themselves inside buildings if given the opportunity.

Brown Rat
■ *Rattus norvegicus*
23cm (43cm including tail)

DESCRIPTION Resembles a scaled-up House Mouse (*above*), but with proportionately smaller eyes and ears. Large-bodied and long-tailed rodent with a heavy, pointed muzzle and rather 'humpbacked' stance. Fur dull brown above, a little paler below but with no clear delineation. Eyes rather small; tail quite thick and blunt-tipped, furless.
DISTRIBUTION Common throughout Europe.
HABITS AND HABITAT Active by night and often by day, all year-round. Supreme opportunist; favours grain and other vegetable foods but eats practically anything, and climbs and swims with ease. Makes burrows in riverbanks; also establishes colonies in buildings. Will breed year-round in many environments, each litter containing usually 7–9 young, but sometimes well into double figures. Commonest in habitats near water, including city sewers.

Rabbit

■ *Oryctolagus cuniculus* 40cm

DESCRIPTION Distinctive short-tailed, long-eared, stocky-bodied mammal. Fur mid-yellow-brown, paler below; black individuals not uncommon. Muzzle short and blunt; eyes large, dark and prominent; ears shaped like long, narrow lily petals. Tail short and broad, black above and white below.
DISTRIBUTION Common in W and S Europe; absent from N Denmark and all but extreme S of Sweden.
HABITS AND HABITAT Partly diurnal. Usually seen grazing in fields. Very social but does not form pair bonds. Breeds and takes shelter in communal burrow system ('warren'), dug by females only in soft earth. Most females have 1 litter of 2–7 a month from late winter to autumn. Runs rapidly for burrow when threatened; signals danger by 'thumping' with hind feet. Open countryside.

Red Squirrel

■ *Sciurus vulgaris*
23cm (40cm including tail)

DESCRIPTION Agile climbing mammal with long, bushy tail. Fur variably red-brown through to almost black above, and white below with clear delineation. Muzzle short, pointed; eyes large, dark; small, round ears often topped with long, thick tufts. Quite long-legged with visible claws. Often sits upright with tail curved against back.
DISTRIBUTION Common across mainland Europe, Scotland and Ireland. Declining in places where Grey Squirrels (p. 47) have been introduced.
HABITS AND HABITAT Diurnal, active year-round. Eats seeds, nuts, invertebrates and bird eggs, foraging in trees and on the ground. Sits up to eat, manipulating food in forepaws. Visits birdfeeders and stores surplus food. Expert climber and jumper. Builds a stick nest in a tree, and has 1 or 2 litters of 2–4. Quite gregarious when foraging. Call is a scolding *chuck chuck*. Woodlands, especially coniferous.

Grey Squirrel
■ *Sciurus carolinensis* 26cm (48cm with tail)

DESCRIPTION Similar to Red Squirrel (p. 46), but bulkier. Fur grey above and white below with no clear delineation, often flushed yellowish around face, forepaws and rump. Tail has a silvery appearance. Has a blunter muzzle than Red Squirrel, and lacks ear tufts.
DISTRIBUTION Introduced to UK. Common in England and Wales, spreading into Scotland and Ireland; also introduced to Italy and spreading N into mainland Europe.
HABITS AND HABITAT Native to North America, but in Europe outcompetes and displaces native Red Squirrel. Similar to Red Squirrel in feeding and breeding habits. Becomes very bold in parks and gardens, visiting birdfeeders and scavenging from bins. Both species strip the scales from pine cones to reach the seeds. Gives a harsh chattering or wheezing call. Found wherever there are trees.

Fox ■ *Vulpes vulpes*
Up to 75cm (120cm including tail)

DESCRIPTION Long-tailed, long-legged, large dog-like predator. Bright or dark orange-red above, white below; white tip to long, bushy tail; blackish legs and paws, sides of muzzle and ears. Muzzle long and pointed, ears pointed and triangular, eyes dark amber. Variable in size, with adult males the largest. Very young cubs are greyish.
DISTRIBUTION Common throughout Europe.
HABITS AND HABITAT Nocturnal, usually shy and unobtrusive. Adaptable and opportunistic; preys on everything from Rabbits (p. 46) and birds to earthworms, though urban Foxes are mostly scavengers and bin-raiders. Surplus food is buried. Pairs form long-term bonds, rearing 4–6 cubs a year in an underground burrow ('earth'). Courting pairs are noisy, with loud barks and screams. Found in all habitats, including city centres.

Badger ■ *Meles meles*
75cm (90cm including tail)

DESCRIPTION Large, stocky, short-legged mammal. Face white with broad black stripes running through eye up to ear. Upperside silver-grey (paler on short, bushy tail), legs and underside from chin to base of tail black. Muzzle long, nose black, eyes dark brown, ears black with white fringe. Paws large and powerful. Varies greatly in size; adult males are largest. DISTRIBUTION Common throughout Europe as far N as central Sweden. HABITS AND HABITAT Nocturnal, and less active in winter months. Highly social, living in complex burrow system ('sett') in groups. Forages on ground, eating roots, fruit, earthworms and any animals it can catch; able to tackle Hedgehogs (p. 41). May damage gardens by digging. Up to 5 cubs are born to the dominant pair of the group in late winter. Woodlands.

Brown Long-eared Bat
■ *Plecotus auritus*
8cm (body), 23cm (wingspan)

DESCRIPTION Small bat with exceptionally long ears. Fur warm mid-brown or grey-brown, paler underneath. Muzzle short, pointed; wings broad; flight slow but manouevrable. Long, broad, blunt-tipped ears almost as long as body, with long, fine tragus. At rest, the ears are often curved back or tucked under a wing. DISTRIBUTION Common across most of Europe, as far N as central Sweden. HABITS AND HABITAT Strictly nocturnal, and hibernates from late autumn to spring. Like other bats, it hunts night-flying insects using echolocation. Roosts and gives birth communally; each female has 1 pup a year, in common with other bats. Woodlands and parks.

Common Pipistrelle

■ *Pipistrellus pipistrellus*
4cm (body), 21cm (wingspan)

DESCRIPTION Smallest, commonest and most urban bat in the region. Dark brown above, barely lighter below. Ears relatively small for a bat, although each is as large as the head, blunt-tipped and almost triangular. Muzzle short and pointed, eyes small. DISTRIBUTION Common across Europe. HABITS AND HABITAT May emerge before nightfall. Flight rapid and jerky; squeak too high for most human ears. Woods and parks; often roosts in buildings. Males defend harems of breeding females. Recently, sound analysis of populations of Common Pipistrelles in the UK has led to the discovery of a new species, the **Soprano Pipistrelle** *P. pygmaeus*, which is virtually identical to the Common but has a consistently higher voice. This species' distribution is now being mapped in mainland Europe.

Common Lizard

■ *Lacerta vivipara* 15cm including tail

DESCRIPTION Slender, long-tailed, short-legged, fairly cylindrical, neckless lizard. Colour variable, but typically dull grey-green with a darker stripe down body sides from snout to tail; underside pale in females, reddish in males. Marked all over with fine dark and light speckles and spots. Snout short and quite blunt; 5 long, slender toes on each foot; small, light brown eyes. DISTRIBUTION Common throughout N and W Europe. HABITS AND HABITAT Diurnal; hibernates. Feeds on insects and other invertebrates, these caught in short dashes. Usually found on the ground but can climb steep surfaces. Spends much time basking in sunshine, although it will quickly dart to cover if disturbed. Females give birth to live young, hence its alternative common name Viviparous Lizard. All habitats with ground cover.

Slow-worm
■ *Anguis fragilis* 40cm

DESCRIPTION Legless lizard, resembling a small, smoothly cylindrical, neckless snake. Colour variable, usually a dull grey-green but may be darker or lighter with more or less prominent longitudinal stripes. Scales small, and body has a polished sheen. Eyes small, dark. Tail often blunt as (in common with other lizards) it breaks off if grabbed by predator.
DISTRIBUTION Common across most of Europe; absent from Ireland and N Sweden.
HABITS AND HABITAT Rarely seen in the open. Hibernates. Feeds on invertebrates, foraging in damp, sheltered places, and is not very swift-moving. Seldom basks, but raises its body temperature by resting in warm places like compost heaps or under metal sheeting. Pairs court in late spring; females give birth to about 8 live young every other year. All well-vegetated habitats.

Grass Snake
■ *Natrix natrix* 100cm

DESCRIPTION Large, graceful snake with an obvious neck. Body dark grey-green with small black bars along flanks at regular intervals. Yellow collar, edged with black and not meeting at back of neck. Top of head green, sides of face black with yellow patches. Eyes orange. N populations are usually more strongly coloured and marked. Females are larger than males.
DISTRIBUTION Common across most of Europe; absent from Ireland, Scotland and N-central Sweden.
HABITS AND HABITAT Mainly diurnal; hibernates. Preys mostly on frogs and toads. Sometimes basks in sunny spots; often swims and may hunt in the water. Courtship occurs in spring, females then laying up to 40 eggs in warm, humid spots like compost heaps. Found in any habitat with good ground cover, usually with water nearby.

Smooth Newt
■ *Triturus vulgaris* 11cm including tail

Male

DESCRIPTION Small, lizard-shaped, smooth-skinned amphibian. Body colour dull green, spotted underneath; tail long and vertically compressed. Breeding males develop bumpy-edged crest along back from neck to tail-tip, and similar frill along bottom edge of tail; also orange coloration on belly and prominent black spots over entire body. Has 5 unwebbed toes on hind feet, 4 on front.

DISTRIBUTION Common across most of Europe; absent from N Sweden.

HABITS AND HABITAT Most active at dusk and dawn. Eats invertebrates. Adults live on land, entering water to breed in spring. After an elaborate courtship, females lay about 300 eggs in the water. The tadpoles have grown limbs by autumn; they breed 2–3 years later. Found in well-vegetated environments close to still, ideally fish-free, ponds and ditches.

Palmate Newt
■ *Triturus helveticus*
9cm including tail

Male

DESCRIPTION Similar to Smooth Newt (*above*), but a little smaller. General coloration very similar but chin and throat always unspotted (spotted in Smooth). Breeding male develops webbing on hind feet, but does not develop crest along body, just a small, smooth-edged crest along tail with small underside frill; underside colouring less intense than on breeding male Smooth Newt.

DISTRIBUTION Fairly common across Great Britain and adjacent mainland Europe; absent from Ireland and Scandinavia.

HABITS AND HABITAT Feeding and breeding behaviour generally similar to Smooth Newt. Like that species, it uses its sticky tongue to trap prey on land. It spends more time in the water than the Smooth Newt, and favours water bodies on acidic soils. Like the Smooth Newt, it hibernates on land, in a sheltered, damp spot such as a rotting woodpile.

Common Frog ▪ *Rana temporaria* 8cm

DESCRIPTION Long-legged, lively, well-marked frog. Body colour typically brownish green with raised darker spots and stripes, and dark mask around eyes. Redder or greener forms not uncommon. Eyes greenish. Outstretched hind legs are as long as the body. Females are larger. Maturing tadpoles are brownish with a golden sheen ('toadpoles' are blacker).
DISTRIBUTION Common throughout most of Europe.
HABITS AND HABITAT Forages on land and in water, catching invertebrate prey with its sticky tongue. Has a croaking call. Hibernates, emerging in spring to spawn in ponds. Male clasps female's back and fertilises eggs as they are released, forming clouds of jelly-like frogspawn. Tadpoles hatch legless and possess long tails for swimming, these gradually receding as their legs develop. Found anywhere near still or slow-moving fresh water.

Common Toad ▪ *Bufo bufo* 12cm

DESCRIPTION Frog-like, but usually larger, less colourful and has warty bumps all over skin. Prominent long swellings (parotoid glands) behind eyes. Usually dull brown or greenish with sparse darker speckles; underside paler. Eyes orange with horizontal pupil.
DISTRIBUTION Common across most of Europe; absent from Ireland.
HABITS AND HABITAT Similar to Common Frog (*above*) in all respects but more terrestrial – adults often found further from water. Less agile and slower-moving, but defends itself by puffing up in an intimidation display; also possesses skin toxins to deter predators. When disturbed, usually walks rather than jumps away. Toadspawn forms long chains rather than amorphous clouds; toadpoles develop skin toxins straight away and so are more often found in ponds with fish than are frog tadpoles. Found in all habitats close to still water.

Large White

■ *Pieris brassicae* 6cm (wingspan)

DESCRIPTION Large white butterfly with blackish body and tips to front wings. Female also has 2 large black spots on front wings. Markings are darker in 2nd-generation butterflies. Underwings flushed yellowish, especially back wings. Slow-flapping but strong flight. Egg yellow, tall and cigar-shaped. Caterpillar yellow with green and black spots. Chrysalis green or brown, attached along its length to vertical surfaces.
DISTRIBUTION Common throughout most of Europe as far N as central Sweden.
HABITS AND HABITAT Nomadic species, found in nearly all habitats. Migrates long distances. Overwinters as a chrysalis – adults emerge in early spring and frequently visit nectar-rich flowers in

Female

gardens. Eggs are laid in groups of 50 or more on cabbages, nasturtiums and related plants. Caterpillars can be quite destructive in vegetable patches. Has 2 generations a year.

Small White

■ *Pieris rapae* 4cm (wingspan)

DESCRIPTION Clearly smaller and more delicate than Large White (*above*). Has a similar pattern, but wing markings are paler and greyer. Male has single dark spot on front wing, female has 2. Egg similar to Large White's but laid singly. Caterpillar green with subtle yellow markings. Chrysalis similar to that of Large White.
DISTRIBUTION Common throughout most of Europe as far N as central Sweden.
HABITS AND HABITAT Nomadic, though a less powerful flyer than Large White. Adults visit nectar-bearing flowers.

Female

Has similar foodplants to Large White, but is less obvious – caterpillar is solitary, and on cabbages remains in the heart of the plant until almost mature. Has 2 generations a year, which may overlap – spring adults emerge from winter chrysalises in early spring, and summer adults emerging in Jun.

Green-veined White

■ *Pieris napi* 4.5cm (wingspan)

DESCRIPTION Has similar wing markings to Small White (p. 53). Dark wing veins are quite prominent on upperside, and are extremely prominent on underside, each broadly overlaid with dark green scales, creating a strong pattern. Egg similar to Small White's. Caterpillar green with row of yellow spots along sides. Chrysalis similar to Small White's. DISTRIBUTION Common and widespread throughout Europe. HABITS AND HABITAT Less nomadic than Small White and less common in town gardens. Adults are active even on dull days, taking nectar frequently. Will also take water from muddy puddles (more common in males). Lays eggs on wild plants of the cabbage family. There are 2 generations a year – adults may be seen any time from Apr to Sep. Found most commonly in damp, low-lying and well-vegetated areas.

Male

Orange Tip

■ *Anthocharis cardamines* 4.5cm (wingspan)

DESCRIPTION Mostly white medium-sized butterfly. Male has broad orange tips to front wings, which are obvious in flight and at rest. Female has greyish tips. Both sexes have heavy moss-green mottling on underside of rear wings. Egg orange, similar in shape to those of other whites. Caterpillar light blue-green. Chrysalis green, attached to plant stem at middle and base and pointing away at tip, like a plant shoot. DISTRIBUTION Common throughout most of Europe. HABITS AND HABITAT Adults emerge from overwintering chrysalis in early spring, soon wandering quite widely in search of nectar and mates. Eggs are laid singly on wild brassicas, especially Cuckoo Flower *Cardamine pratensis*; caterpillar eats the flower buds rather than the leaves. Usually has only 1 generation a year. Open woodlands and well-vegetated countryside generally.

Brimstone

■ *Gonepteryx rhamni* 6.5cm (wingspan)

Male

DESCRIPTION Large butterfly with distinctive pointed wingtips. Each wing has a small brownish spot near centre, otherwise bright butter-yellow (male) or creamy greenish white (female). Wings rarely held open when resting. Egg tall and narrow, yellowish. Caterpillar smooth and green. Leaf-shaped chrysalis attached to a plant stem and an overhanging leaf.
DISTRIBUTION Common across most of Europe; absent from N Scotland and N Sweden.
HABITS AND HABITAT Overwinters in adult form, emerging from hibernation on the first warm days of spring and wandering in search of a mate. Eggs are laid on Buckthorn *Rhamnus cathartica* and Alder Buckthorn *Frangula alnus*. The next generation emerges in summer and does not mate, instead concentrating on feeding to lay down fat for hibernation. Often hibernates in clumps of Ivy (p. 117). Strong flyer. Woodlands and open, scrubby countryside.

Clouded Yellow

■ *Colias croceus* 5.5cm (wingspan)

DESCRIPTION Bright orange-yellow butterfly, with broad blackish borders to all inner wings (chequered with yellow in female) and single dark spot on forewings. Underside also yellow, with white spot on hindwings. Egg like Large White's (p. 53). Caterpillar green with yellow stripe along flanks. Chrysalis pale green, more squat than those of other whites.
DISTRIBUTION Immigrant from S Europe and N Africa, adults migrating N in summer in very variable numbers.
HABITS AND HABITAT Strong flyer with a powerful migratory instinct. In good years, thousands reach N Europe and seek out clover-rich fields, where they lay their eggs, producing a new autumn generation (however, none survives the N European winter). Most often seen in open habitats. Adults stop to feed from flowers frequently, always closing their wings at rest.

Small Tortoiseshell
▪ *Aglais urticae* 5.5cm (wingspan)

DESCRIPTION Medium-sized, colourful butterfly. Inner wings orange-red with dark bases and borders, upperwings marked with large black and pale yellow spots. Borders contain row of bright blue spots. Outer wings dark and cryptic, providing camouflage. Egg a squat green cylinder. Caterpillar dark, spiny. Chrysalis brown, like a dead leaf, suspended by tip.
DISTRIBUTION Common throughout Europe.
HABITS AND HABITAT Strong-flying, nomadic. Hibernates in outbuildings or other sheltered spots, flying on first sunny spring days to seek a mate. Courtship takes place by Stinging Nettle (p. 117) beds, where eggs are laid in groups on undersides of leaves. Caterpillars live in communal silk web when small, dispersing when mature. Summer adults produce an autumn generation, which feeds on nectar from flowers like Buddleia (p. 114) and also from windfall fruit before hibernation.

Painted Lady
▪ *Cynthia cardui* 6.5cm (wingspan)

DESCRIPTION Large; inner wings mainly salmon-pink with white-spotted black tips and black spots along border of hindwing. Underside pale brown, somewhat cryptic with row of eye-spots along hindwing border. Egg a squat green cylinder, becoming grey. Caterpillar greyish with white tufts of hair. Chrysalis brown, suspended by tip on leaf underside.
DISTRIBUTION Immigrant from Africa, reaching Europe in varying numbers from spring.
HABITS AND HABITAT Strong-flying, nomadic and migratory species. In some years it can be extremely numerous in N Europe. Adults lay eggs on thistles, giving rise to a new generation; this does not survive the N winter, though it is thought that many migrate southwards again. Frequently visits flowers for nectar and also basks in the sun, flying off powerfully when disturbed.

Red Admiral

■ *Vanessa atalanta* 7.5cm (wingspan)

DESCRIPTION Large and striking. Inner wings mainly dark with broad red band across both and white spots at tip of forewing. Underside dark, with red and white on forewing (concealed in normal resting posture). Egg a ridged green cylinder, laid singly. Caterpillar has long spines, its colour varying from black to pale greenish. Chrysalis grey with gold spots, suspended by tip. DISTRIBUTION Resident across most of Europe, numbers boosted by migrants from further S. HABITS AND HABITAT Overwinters as an adult, appearing on fine spring days. Strong flyer – most of those seen in N Europe in summer are immigrants. Eggs laid on Stinging Nettle (p. 117); caterpillar makes tent from nettle leaf when small. Adults in summer feed avidly on nectar, and are also attracted to windfall fruit. Hibernates in sheltered spots, including outbuildings.

Peacock

■ *Inachis io* 7cm (wingspan)

DESCRIPTION Very striking, large, colourful butterfly. Inner wings rich burgundy-red with large blue, yellow and black eye-spots on the top outer section of each. Underside plain blackish brown. Egg a squat yellowish cylinder, laid in clusters. Caterpillar blackish, spiny. Chrysalis yellow or greyish, suspended by tip. DISTRIBUTION Common across most of Europe, becoming scarce in Scotland and N Sweden. HABITS AND HABITAT Life cycle and behaviour very similar in all respects to that of Small Tortoiseshell

(p. 56). Gardeners wishing to attract these species and Red Admirals (*above*) should maintain a patch of Stinging Nettles (p. 117) in a partly sunny, partly shaded situation, as well as cultivate nectar-rich flowers. The adult's eye-spots are used to startle predators – the butterfly can also make a scraping noise by rubbing its wings together.

Comma ■ *Polygonia c-album*
5.5cm (wingspan)

DESCRIPTION Medium-sized orange butterfly with distinctive ragged-looking wing edges. Inner wings orange with dark edges and spots; outer wings dull greyish (darker in later generations), with small white comma-shaped mark on hindwing. Egg a squat green cylinder. Caterpillar greenish with white rear end, resembling a bird dropping. Chrysalis hanging, brown, resembling a dead leaf.

DISTRIBUTION Common across most of Europe; scarcer in Scotland and N Scandinavia; absent from Ireland.

HABITS AND HABITAT Less inclined to wander than related species like Small Tortoiseshell (p. 56). Hibernating adults emerge in spring. Has 2 generations a year, the 2nd of which hibernates. Eggs are laid in small clusters on Hop *Humulus lupulus*, Stinging Nettle (p. 117) or currant leaves; the caterpillar is solitary. Adults are territorial, defending their favourite basking spots from other butterflies. Likes sheltered, well-vegetated spots.

Male

Purple Hairstreak
■ *Neozephyrus quercus*
3.5cm (wingspan)

DESCRIPTION Small, with short, pointed tails on hindwings. Inner wings dark with patches of purple sheen (extensive in male, on forewings only in female). Outer wings pale grey with dark-edged whitish line from top to bottom. Egg whitish, bun-shaped. Caterpillar short-bodied, flattened, woodlouse-like. Chrysalis brown, smooth and roundish, formed on the ground.

DISTRIBUTION Common across most of Europe; only in S of Ireland, Scotland and Sweden.

HABITS AND HABITAT Eggs are laid on oak twigs, and adults rarely stray far from oaks, mainly flying around treetops and feeding on honeydew excreted by aphids on leaf surfaces, but sometimes descending to feed from flowers. Caterpillars hatch in spring and eat young oak leaves, pupating on the ground – adults emerge in late Jun. Oak woodlands.

Holly Blue

■ *Celastrina argiolus* 3cm (wingspan)

DESCRIPTION The blue butterfly most likely to visit gardens. Inner wings bright violet-blue, with narrow black fringes (broader in females, especially those of the 2nd generation). Outer wings pale silver-blue, with scattered small black spots. Egg blue-green, bun-shaped. Caterpillar green, squat, flattened. Chrysalis rounded, brownish, attached to underside of foodplant leaf.
DISTRIBUTION Common throughout most of Europe; scattered in Ireland; mostly absent from Scotland.
HABITS AND HABITAT 1st-generation

Female

adults emerge from their chrysalises in early spring. Eggs are laid on Holly (1st generation; p. 111) or Ivy (2nd; p. 117) – caterpillars feed on the flower buds, which mature at different times in the 2 species. Adults visit flowers for nectar and also sip water from puddles or pond edges, rarely opening wings when resting. Gardens, woods and hedgerows.

Lime Hawkmoth

■ *Mimas tiliae* 6.5cm (wingspan)

DESCRIPTION Adult has long, quite narrow wings with wavy edges, plump body. Wings dusky pink with darker greenish-brown markings; held at 45 degrees to body, leaving abdomen exposed. Sides of thorax dark, centre paler. Egg round, green. Larva has horn at tail-tip; green with narrow yellow stripes, greyish when mature. Pupa brown, formed inside crack in tree bark.
DISTRIBUTION Common across much of Europe; not in Scotland or N Scandinavia.
HABITS AND HABITAT Overwinters as pupa, emerging May–Jun. Nocturnal, attracted to light; does not feed. Eggs are laid singly or in pairs on leaves of lime trees, also sometimes on elms and alders. Caterpillars feed alone on leaves, and move off from feeding areas when mature to pupate. Found wherever suitable trees grow.

Poplar Hawkmoth

■ *Laothoe populi* 7cm (wingspan)

DESCRIPTION Large, with striking posture at rest – forewings half-spread, but hindwings fully spread so their outer edges are exposed. Abdomen very plump. Various shades of brown, with reddish patches on concealed parts of hindwings. Egg green, round. Caterpillar green with tail horn, developing red spots and yellow stripes with age. Pupa formed just underground, blackish, smooth.

DISTRIBUTION Common across Europe, becoming scarcer in more northerly areas.

HABITS AND HABITAT 2 generations fly each year, so may be seen May–Aug. Nocturnal, attracted to light; rests on tree trunks by day. Eggs are laid on the undersides of poplar leaves, also willows, Sallow *Salix caprea* and Aspen *Populus tremula*. Mature caterpillars may be found on the ground. Found wherever foodplant trees grow, especially close to rivers.

Eyed Hawkmoth

■ *Smerinthus ocellata* 7cm (wingspan)

DESCRIPTION Superficially similar to Lime Hawkmoth (p. 59), with similar resting posture, but upperwings have pinkish wash, and more intricate and subtle pattern. Thorax has pale sides and broad blackish stripe down centre. Large, black-centred blue eye-spots on pinkish green. Caterpillar horn-tailed, yellow-green with whitish stripes. Pupa formed in soil near surface, blackish brown and smooth.

DISTRIBUTION Common across most of Europe; absent from most of Scotland and N Scandinavia.

HABITS AND HABITAT Adults fly in late spring, sometimes with a 2nd summer brood. Nocturnal, feeding on flower nectar and resting in concealed spots by day. Eggs are laid on willow, Apple *Malus domestica* and other tree leaves; caterpillars eat leaves until fully grown, when they wander off to find pupation spots. Woods, orchards and gardens.

Privet Hawkmoth

■ *Sphinx ligustri* 11.5cm (wingspan)

DESCRIPTION Very large, heavy-bodied and long-winged – wings usually held fully closed over body at rest. Forewings have subtle brown pattern, pinkish at base. Hindwings and abdomen banded pink and blackish, thorax blackish. Egg round, green. Caterpillar green, horn-tailed, developing pink-edged white stripes. Becomes browner when fully mature. Pupa buried in soil, brown or brownish black.

DISTRIBUTION Common across most of Europe; not Ireland, Scotland or N Sweden.

HABITS AND HABITAT Adults emerge from the pupae in midsummer. Nocturnal, feeding in flight from flowers like Honeysuckle (p. 116); also attracted to light. Foodplants include Common Privet (p. 115), lilacs and various native trees. Mature caterpillars wander to find soft soil in which to burrow and pupate – pupal stage may last 2 years. Scrubland, parks and gardens.

Elephant Hawkmoth

■ *Deilephila elpenor* 6cm (wingspan)

DESCRIPTION Distinctive moth. Body and wings attractively patterned in pink and soft moss-green. Underside very bright pink. Legs, antennae and edges of inner forewings white; hindwings blackish at base. Body broad, tapering sharply to a point. Egg round, green. Caterpillar horn-tailed, usually grey-brown with eye-spots near head; tapers at head but can greatly expand this end when threatened, enlarging eye-spots. Pupa formed in soil, brownish grey.

DISTRIBUTION Common across most of Europe, not reaching N Scandinavia.

HABITS AND HABITAT Nocturnal; adults fly in Jun and feed from various nectar-rich flowers. Eggs are laid on willowherbs, also sometimes fuchsias and related plants. Mature caterpillars wander on the ground to find suitable soft soil in which to pupate. Waste ground, scrubland, parks and gardens.

Puss Moth ■ *Cerura vinula*
6cm (wingspan)

DESCRIPTION Adult pale, furry; grey or whitish wings with fine dark speckles and zigzag markings. Body thick, with grey bands. Male's antennae feathery, female's fine. Egg squat, reddish. Caterpillar has long, thin double 'tails'; black when young; green with black back and white side-stripe when mature, and when alarmed shows extraordinary pink and black 'face' markings at enlarged head end. Pupa almost round, hard, blackish, formed within tree bark. DISTRIBUTION Common throughout Europe. HABITS AND HABITAT Adults fly Apr–Jul. Nocturnal, attracted to light. Eggs laid on Sallow *Salix caprea*, willows and poplars. Mature caterpillars rely on striking threat display to deter rather than camouflage, producing whip-like flagellae from the 'tails' and rearing up to display the 'face' – they can also squirt formic acid. Damp, wooded habitats.

Buff-tip ■ *Phalera bucephala*
5cm (wingspan)

DESCRIPTION At rest, adult holds wings down to create cylindrical shape. Patterned to resemble broken Silver Birch twig (p. 109), with buffish wing-tips and head, and wings otherwise silvery grey with fine dark and light markings. Egg blackish. Caterpillar yellow-white with black head and black markings on each segment. Pupa is formed underground, dark purplish or blackish. DISTRIBUTION Common throughout Europe. HABITS AND HABITAT Adults fly at night in May–Jul. They are somewhat attracted to light. Eggs are laid in clusters on leaves of a variety of plants, including Aspen *Populus tremula*, Sallow *Salix caprea*, whitebeams, fruit trees, oaks and Hazel *Corylus avellana*. Caterpillars feed gregariously when small, and can completely defoliate young saplings. Mature caterpillars wander off to pupate in soil. Found in many habitats, wherever suitable foodplants grow.

Chocolate-tip

■ *Clostera curtula* 3cm (wingspan)

DESCRIPTION Silvery moth with fine white lines across wings. Head, thorax and wing-tips dark chocolate-brown. Shape at rest distinctive, with furry forelegs thrust forward, wings rolled to make a cylinder shape; abdomen tip reaching beyond wing-tips and often tilted up. Male antennae very feathery. Egg round, greenish blue. Caterpillar hairy and dark, becoming paler with orange and black speckles. Pupa glossy, fixed with silk in leaf shelter.

DISTRIBUTION Common across Europe.

HABITS AND HABITAT Has 2 broods a year: Apr–May and Aug–Sep (just 1 midsummer brood in N parts). Nocturnal, attracted to light and nectar-bearing flowers. Eggs laid in clusters on willows, poplars and other trees. Caterpillars pupate on leaf, and winter is spent in this stage. Found in wooded areas where suitable foodplants grow.

Iron Prominent

■ *Notodonta dromedarius* 4cm (wingspan)

DESCRIPTION Wings dull, dark grey with reddish and buff bands and mottling, like rusty patches on iron. Darker in the N of its range. Hindwings pale, but normally covered by forewings at rest. Egg round, light green. Caterpillar variably greenish or brown; a fleshy and nearly hairless, humped shape with short, blunt projections on upperside, becoming more striking as it matures. Pupa squat, glossy chestnut-brown; formed in soil.

DISTRIBUTION Fairly common throughout Europe, becoming scarcer further N.

HABITS AND HABITAT Nocturnal. Has 2 generations in the S (adults flying May–Jun and Aug–Sep), 1 in the N (Jun–Jul). Adults are attracted to light. Eggs are usually laid on birches, and also sometimes on other tree species. Found in sheltered wooded areas in proximity to its preferred foodplants.

Swallow Prominent
■ *Pheosia tremula* 5cm (wingspan)

DESCRIPTION Mainly grey and white moth with a ridged thorax. Wings dark along edges and close to body, with broad, pale wedge down middle. N populations are paler. At rest, wings are swept back, their outer edges appearing parallel from above. Egg squat, whitish. Caterpillar green (sometimes brown) with yellow stripe down side, and hump close to tail end. Pupa formed in leaf litter; shiny, dark brown.
DISTRIBUTION Common across most of Europe; scarcer in Ireland, Scotland and N Sweden.
HABITS AND HABITAT Nocturnal, quite strongly attracted to light. 2 generations of adults fly each year in S regions (May–Jun and Aug), just 1 further N (May–Jun). Eggs are laid singly on willow or poplar leaves. Mature caterpillars descend to pupate among leaf litter or in shallow soil. Parks and gardens.

Lesser Swallow Prominent
■ *Pheosia gnoma* 5cm (wingspan)

DESCRIPTION Very similar to Swallow Prominent (*above*), but very slightly smaller, with the same swept-back wings in typical resting posture, ridged thorax and basic colour scheme. Main distinguishing feature is the white wedge on the inner lower edge of the forewing; this is also present in the Swallow Prominent but is more obscure and much less noticeable in that species. Underwing pattern is also slightly different, although this is hard to observe in the field. Egg and pupa similar to those of Swallow Prominent; caterpillar greyer, with broader and more distinct yellow stripe.
DISTRIBUTION Fairly common across most of Europe.
HABITS AND HABITAT Ecologically very similar to Swallow Prominent, with the same flying seasons. Eggs are laid on birch leaves, and the species pupates in leaf litter or just under the soil surface. Parks, gardens and woodland.

Pale Tussock

■ *Calliteara pudibunda* 5cm (wingspan)

DESCRIPTION Light-coloured, very hairy moth. Wings pale grey or off-white with fine grey-brown bands and vermiculations. A dark variant is sometimes seen, most commonly in industrial areas. Front legs very hairy, held thrust forwards. Male antennae feathery. Egg round, whitish. Caterpillar pale green or yellowish, with long bristles on sides, dense tufts of upright yellow hairs on uppersides of 4 segments near head end, and a brown tail tuft. Pupates inside silk cocoon in leaf litter. DISTRIBUTION Widespread across Europe; rare in Ireland and absent from Scotland and N Sweden. HABITS AND HABITAT Adults fly in May–Jun. Nocturnal, attracted to light; does not feed. Eggs are laid in large clusters on oaks, willows and deciduous plants. Found in parks, gardens, orchards and woodland.

Garden Tiger

■ *Arctia caja* 6cm (wingspan)

DESCRIPTION Colourful, unmistakable moth. Upperwings dark chocolate-brown, broken into blotches by uneven creamy-white stripes; furry thorax also chocolate-brown. Underwings bright scarlet with large black, dark blue-centred spots; abdomen banded red and blackish. Egg round, greenish white. Caterpillar completely covered in long hairs; white and black on upperside, shading to red-brown on sides. Pupa glossy brown within silk cocoon, formed in leaf litter. DISTRIBUTION Common and widespread across most of Europe. HABITS AND HABITAT Adults fly at

night in Jul and Aug. They lay clusters of eggs on various herbaceous plants, including Strawberry *Fragaria × ananassa*, Dandelion (p. 146), docks and dead-nettles. 'Woolly bear' caterpillars are protected from predators by their long hair, and may be seen feeding in exposed situations. Gardens and other situations where the foodplants grow.

White Ermine
■ *Spilosoma lubricipeda*
4cm (wingspan)

DESCRIPTION White moth with very furry thorax and legs. Wings speckled with scattered small black dots, not forming an obvious pattern. Eyes, lower parts of legs and antennae also dark; male antennae comb-like. Egg glossy, pale yellowish. Caterpillar dark, covered in short, dark hairs and with dark red stripe along back. Squat, smooth blackish pupa is formed within thick silk cocoon, among leaf litter.
DISTRIBUTION Common across most of Europe, but not in far N.
HABITS AND HABITAT Adults fly at night in late May–Jul. They are distasteful to predators so often rest in exposed situations. Eggs are laid in groups on the undersides of leaves – foodplants include Dandelions (p. 146), docks, nettles and many other plants. Winters as a pupa. Gardens and woodlands.

Buff Ermine
■ *Spilosoma luteum* 3.5cm

DESCRIPTION Superficially similar to White Ermine (*above*), but wing ground colour is a warm creamy-buff colour. Arrangement of dark spots variable, but they often form a distinct pattern with a straight line across wings just below thorax, and an inverted V-shape below that, with other spots scattered on outer edges of wings. Egg and pupa similar to those of White Ermine; caterpillar paler (especially in early stages) with less distinct red stripe.
DISTRIBUTION Common across most of Europe except far N.
HABITS AND HABITAT Nocturnal; adults fly in Jun and Jul. Ecology similar to White Ermine. It is thought to be a Batesian mimic of White Ermine, flying a little later and benefiting from predators' learned avoidance of that species, and is not distasteful itself. Wasteland and gardens.

The Cinnabar

■ *Tyria jacobaeae* 4cm (wingspan)

DESCRIPTION Very distinctive red and black moth. Forewings black with broad red stripes along outer edge and 2 red spots on lower edge. Underwings red with narrow outer black border. Egg round, yellow. Caterpillar sparsely hairy, banded alternately bright orange and black with black head. Pupa formed in thin silk cocoon in leaf litter or just under soil surface.
DISTRIBUTION Common across most of Europe, becoming rare or absent in N areas.
HABITS AND HABITAT Flies in the daytime and also at night. Poisonous to predators in all forms. Adults are on the wing from May to mid-Jul. Eggs are laid in clusters on Common Ragwort leaves (p. 144), and caterpillars feed conspicuously and gregariously on the leaves through late summer, pupating over winter. Waste ground and pastures.

Heart and Dart

■ *Agrotis exclamationis*
3.5cm (wingspan)

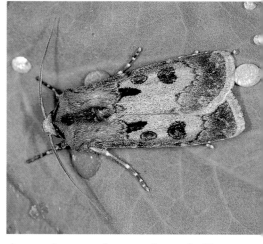

DESCRIPTION Grey-brown moth with distinctive dark markings on forewings: large, circular central mark ('heart'); and short, dark streak above, reaching up to thorax ('dart'). Wings otherwise finely and subtly patterned with dark and light bands and scallops. Viewed head-on, shows a dark line across thorax. Underwings pale. Early life stages rarely seen.
DISTRIBUTION Common and widespread across Europe.
HABITS AND HABITAT Adults fly by night in 1 (N areas) or 2 (more southerly areas) generations, the 1st in May and Jun and the 2nd, where it occurs, in Jul and Aug. Eggs are laid on the ground or on very low parts of assorted wild and garden plants – caterpillars remain close to the ground and well hidden, pupating in soil. Gardens, parks, wasteland and woodland.

Hebrew Character
■ *Orthosia gothica* 3.5cm (wingspan)

DESCRIPTION Dark grey and brown moth, with a blackish, vaguely L-shaped marking on the centre of each forewing, along with other more subtle light and dark markings. N populations are paler. Furry, with long antennae. Eggs round, whitish. Caterpillar pinkish when small, becoming green with white stripes down back and sides. Pupa shiny, dark brown, formed in leaf litter. DISTRIBUTION Widespread and common across Europe.

HABITS AND HABITAT An early-flying species, emerging in Mar and on the wing at night through Apr (later in N of its region). Often feeds on flowers of Sallow *Salix caprea*, and is attracted to light. Eggs are laid in clusters on a wide variety of woody and herbaceous plants. Overwinters as a pupa. Found in most habitat types.

Broad-bordered Yellow Underwing
■ *Noctua fimbriata* 5cm (wingspan)

DESCRIPTION Large moth with dull, camouflaged forewings (considerably darker in males), held tightly closed at rest, and brighter hindwings, revealed when resting moth

is startled. Forewings have vague, dark-centred light circular marking at centre, and lighter border. Hindwings bright yellow with broad, dark border. Egg dome-shaped, pale. Caterpillar dull yellowish with row of dark spots down sides. Pupa shiny brown, formed underground. DISTRIBUTION Common across most of Europe, becoming scarcer into N Scotland and Sweden. HABITS AND HABITAT Flies at night in 1 generation, emerging in Jul. Eggs are laid in large clusters (up to 1,000) on a wide variety of low-growing plants, which the caterpillars feed on at night. They pupate underground in Apr. Found in most habitats, especially woodland.

Large Yellow Underwing
■ *Noctua pronuba* 5cm (wingspan)

DESCRIPTION Similar to Broad-bordered
Yellow Underwing (p. 68), but forewings
greyer, with distinct dark mark on leading
border close to wing-tips. Males usually
darker. Other forewing markings vague and
variable. Underwings yellow with narrower
black border. Rests with wings tightly
closed. Egg domed, yellowish. Caterpillar
smooth, green with pale and dark stripes
along sides; also occurs in brown form. Pupa
formed underground, glossy brown-black.
DISTRIBUTION Common and widespread
across Europe.
HABITS AND HABITAT Nocturnal, on the
wing from late Jun into Oct. Adults feed on flowers and are attracted to light. Foodplants
include various grasses as well as other low-growing plants. The caterpillar feeds at night
through winter, resting on the ground on the coldest nights, and pupates in mid-spring.
May be seen in almost any habitat.

Bright-line Brown-eye
■ *Lacanobia oleracea* 3.5cm (wingspan)

DESCRIPTION Dark moth, which
normally holds wings over body in
V-shape. Forewings have clear whitish
line across their width, close to edge, and
distinct pale-circled brown marking above.
Underwings whitish. Egg dome-shaped,
pale green. Caterpillar green or brown,
smooth-bodied, and with obvious broad
yellow line down sides. Pupa glossy
red-brown, formed underground.
DISTRIBUTION Common and widespread
across most of Europe. Rarer or absent in
N Scotland and Scandinavia.
HABITS AND HABITAT Nocturnal.
In most of its range it has 1 brood a year,
adults flying May–Jul. A 2nd autumn brood
may appear in the S. Eggs are laid on orache and goosefoot species, sometimes also on
cultivated tomatoes. The caterpillar feeds at night and stays quite close to the ground.
It pupates in soil. Most common in damp wooded habitats.

Common Wainscot
■ *Mythimna pallens* 3cm (wingspan)

DESCRIPTION Undistinguished moth with plain, unpatterned wings. Usually whitish but may have a buff or pinkish wash. Wing veins prominent. Thorax light brown, hairy. Legs relatively long and hairless. Egg a squat, pale disc. Caterpillar tapered at both ends, smooth-bodied with sparse hair, brown with dark and pale lines down back and sides. Pupa glossy, dark, formed within leaf litter.

DISTRIBUTION Widespread across most of Europe, becoming scarcer further N.

HABITS AND HABITAT One of many similar species. Has 2 broods a year across most of its range, so may be seen from mid-spring into autumn. Nocturnal, visiting flowers and also coming to light. Caterpillars feed by night on various grass species, including Cocksfoot *Dactylis glomerata* and couch grasses, hiding within the grass tussock by day. Grassy habitats.

Satellite
■ *Eupsilia transversa* 3.5cm (wingspan)

DESCRIPTION Dark, warm brown moth. Most striking feature is a whitish, yellow-white or yellow-orange round spot at the centre of each forewing, though on worn individuals this may be difficult to discern. Forewings otherwise subtly banded and scalloped. Hindwings dusky grey. Egg dome-shaped. Caterpillar dark greyish brown with white line low down along sides. Pupa glossy brown, formed in the earth.

DISTRIBUTION Common over much of Europe, becoming scarcer further N.

HABITS AND HABITAT Nocturnal, attracted to light and night-scented flowers. Adults emerge late in the year and may be seen anytime from Sep through to the following spring. Eggs are laid on various deciduous trees, and caterpillars may consume other moth larvae as well as foodplant leaves – they can even bite a human finger. Most habitats.

Poplar Grey
■ *Acronicta megacephala* 4cm (wingspan)

DESCRIPTION Very furry grey moth, with subtle but attractive patterning. Usually shows a distinct pale, circular mark with a darker centre on middle of forewings, and alternate greyish and whitish scalloped banding across rest of forewings. Underwings plain whitish. Legs banded alternately light and dark grey. Egg a flattened dome, greenish. Caterpillar grey-greenish with dark and light speckles, rather sparse but very long hairs, and a relatively large head. Pupa bright red-brown. DISTRIBUTION Common and widespread across most of Europe, but scarcer in far N.
HABITS AND HABITAT Nocturnal moth, flying May–Jun. Lays eggs on poplars and Aspen *Populus tremula*. Caterpillar feeds at night, resting with head curled back in 'question mark' shape in the day. Found in woodlands and other habitats where the foodplants grow.

Grey Dagger
■ *Acronicta psi* 3.5cm (wingspan)

DESCRIPTION Dagger-like black streaks down cold mid-grey forewings from thorax, and discontinuously from halfway down to edge of forewings. Hindwings dull whitish. Body and legs also grey, with dark bands on legs. Very similar to Dark Dagger *A. tridens*. Egg a flattened dome. Caterpillar black with white underside and broad yellow stripe down back, red spots along sides; has black projection on back close to head end, and similar but shorter projection at tail end. Pupa glossy red-brown.
DISTRIBUTION Common across much of Europe; not N Scotland or N Sweden.
HABITS AND HABITAT Nocturnal. Has 1 brood a year, on the wing Jun–Aug. It lays eggs on plants such as Apple *Malus domestica*, Beech *Fagus sylvatica*, oaks and willows. The caterpillars pupate underground. Woodlands, orchards, parks and gardens.

Nut-tree Tussock
■ *Colocasia coryli* 4cm (wingspan)

DESCRIPTION Very hairy moth, quite variable in its basic coloration though not in pattern. Forewings darkest close to body, with indistinct darker, circular markings. Broad, paler band begins abruptly halfway down wing length, gradually darkening towards wing edge with subtle banding. Long greyish hair on legs and body. Egg round, pale. Caterpillar black when small, becoming light brown with dark stripes, and covered in tufts of long hair. Pupa brown, formed on ground within cocoon.
DISTRIBUTION Widespread across Europe, becoming scarce into N Scotland and N Sweden.
HABITS AND HABITAT Nocturnal. 2 generations fly in the S (Apr–May and Jul–Sep) and 1 in the N (May–Jun). Attracted to light. Eggs are laid on Hazel *Corylus avellana*, Hornbeam *Carpinus betulus*, birches and other deciduous trees. Woodland and scrubby habitats.

Old Lady
■ *Mormo maura* 6cm (wingspan)

DESCRIPTION Large, dark, broad-winged moth. Wings intricately patterned in various greys and browns, forewings with dark area in centre and paler edge. Underwings also dull and cryptic. Egg round, ridged. Caterpillar grey-brown with sparse, short hairs; becomes plump when mature, with body much wider than head, and faint, pale line down sides and row of small orange spots. Pupa brown, plump; formed within bark crevice.
DISTRIBUTION Widespread but patchily distributed in Europe; rare in N.
HABITS AND HABITAT Nocturnal, not drawn to light but comes to scented flowers. Flies in 1 generation, Jul–Aug. By day may roost in groups, in sheltered spots, sometimes in sheds or outbuildings. Usual foodplant is Blackthorn *Prunus spinosa*, although others may also be used. Damp, sheltered woodland or scrubby habitats.

Angle Shades
■ *Phlogophora meticulosa* 4.5cm (wingspan)

DESCRIPTION Unusual-looking moth that rests
with its wings rolled over at the edges, giving
it the appearance of a withered leaf. Mainly
light greyish; blackish V-shaped marking with
dark pinkish centre on side of each forewing,
resembling half a large eye-spot. Wing edges
uneven. Long-legged. Egg pinkish, round and
ridged. Caterpillar green with whitish side-stripe.
Pupa glossy brown, in loose silk cocoon just under
soil surface.

DISTRIBUTION Common across most of Europe;
not Ireland, N Scotland or N Sweden.

HABITS AND HABITAT Nocturnal. On the wing
from May to Oct in 2 generations, supplemented
by migrants from further S. Eggs are laid on a
wide variety of woody and herbaceous plants.
Overwinters as a caterpillar. Found in many
different types of habitat.

Burnished Brass
■ *Diachrysia chrysitis* 3cm (wingspan)

DESCRIPTION Strikingly coloured
and shaped moth. Wings gleaming
greenish, iridescent, with band of dark
brown across centre (sometimes solid,
sometimes broken). Has a broad fan of
erect hairs forming a crest on thorax.
Underwings dull grey. Egg round, pale
green, ridged. Caterpillar green with
yellow line down side; body broad and
plump at tail end, tapering towards
head end. Pupa blackish and shiny,
formed in foodplant leaves.

DISTRIBUTION Common across most
of Europe, becoming scarcer in far N.

HABITS AND HABITAT Usually

nocturnal. Has 1 or 2 generations a year, and in S may be seen from May to Sep. Feeds on
flowers and lays eggs on various common wayside plants, including dead-nettles, Stinging
Nettle (p. 117) and Common Burdock *Arctium minus*. Caterpillar spends the winter
sheltering in foodplant leaves, pupating in spring. Gardens and hedgerows.

Herald ■ *Scoliopteryx libatrix* 4cm (wingspan)

DESCRIPTION Attractive and distinctive brown moth. Has a white or cream line across forewing at the one-third point and another at the two-thirds point – the lower line is double. Forewings and thorax are patterned with large patches of bright, gleaming chestnut. Wing edges uneven and scalloped. Egg round, pale green. Caterpillar light, bright green, almost hairless, with dark-edged white stripe down side. Pupa shiny, dark, formed inside silk cocoon between 2 leaves in leaf litter.
DISTRIBUTION Common and widespread across Europe.
HABITS AND HABITAT Nocturnal. Adults fly from late Jul to Nov, hibernate, and then re-emerge the following Mar. They are attracted to light and flowers, and also to ripe blackberries in autumn. They may hibernate inside outbuildings. Eggs are laid on willows, Aspen *Populus tremula* and poplars. Woodlands and scrubby habitats.

Silver Y ■ *Autographa gamma* 4cm (wingspan)

DESCRIPTION Grey-brown moth with tuft of hair on thorax. Forewings have white Y-shaped marking like Greek character *gamma* with blackish surround (hence its scientific name), otherwise wings finely and subtly patterned in various shades of grey. Egg round, whitish. Caterpillar green with yellow stripes down back and sides. Pupa dark grey-brown, formed in loose silk cocoon within a curled-up dead leaf.
DISTRIBUTION Found throughout Europe; in N countries population is comprised of migrants from further S.
HABITS AND HABITAT Active day and night, and may be seen from spring through to autumn, buzzing clumsily around flowers to feed. Also comes to light. Throughout N Europe it does breed, but caterpillars seldom, if ever, survive through the winter. Foodplants include Stinging Nettle (p. 117), Bramble (p. 125) and clovers. May be found in almost any habitat.

Beautiful Golden Y
■ *Autographa pulchrina* 3.5cm (wingspan)

DESCRIPTION Similar to Silver Y (p. 74), but
forewings usually darker, often richer reddish
brown, and more strongly patterned with whitish
or yellow wing marking consisting of a hook
shape with a spot underneath. Hindwings dull
grey-brown. Early stages very similar to those
of Silver Y.

DISTRIBUTION Widespread and common
across Europe, becoming scarcer in far N.

HABITS AND HABITAT Adults are nocturnal,
and fly in a single generation from Jun to Jul. They
are attracted to nectar-bearing flowers and also to
light. Eggs are laid on a wide range of foodplants,
including birches, dead-nettles, Honeysuckle
(p. 116), Common Ragwort (p. 144) and Rowan
(p. 112), and the caterpillars overwinter before
pupating the following spring, in a cocoon formed
on their foodplant. Favours sheltered habitats,
including woodland, hedgerows and gardens.

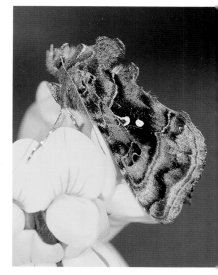

The Spectacle
■ *Abrostola tripartita* 3cm (wingspan)

DESCRIPTION Rather dark, dull grey moth with
tufts of hair on thorax. When viewed head-on,
the nearest raised thorax hairs resemble a pair
of spectacles. Forewings grey-brown with more
or less subtle lighter and darker markings. Egg
round. Caterpillar grey-greenish, humped and
small-headed, with white stripe down side and
white stripes on each segment. Pupa formed
among leaf litter, dark brown.

DISTRIBUTION Fairly common and widespread
across Europe, becoming scarcer in the far N.

HABITS AND HABITAT Adults fly by night
in 1 or 2 generations, often coming to light.
The foodplant is the Stinging Nettle (p. 117),
and the caterpillar can be seen resting among
nettle leaves in late summer. It pupates in autumn
among the leaf litter. Occurs in a wide variety of
habitats, wherever Stinging Nettles are plentiful.

Red Underwing
▪ *Catocala nupta* 7cm (wingspan)

DESCRIPTION Large moth with broad, butterfly-like wings. Forewings a rather uniform mid-grey-brown, with subtle fine bands and scalloping. Hindwings, revealed when resting moth is startled, are bright crimson with broad black border and broad black C-shaped mark halfway up. Egg round, ridged. Caterpillar dark or light brown, relatively long and slender. Pupa formed in cocoon in leaf litter. DISTRIBUTION Widespread and common across much of Europe, but not reaching Scotland or N Sweden. HABITS AND HABITAT Nocturnal, attracted to light and feeds from flowers. On the wing in Aug and Sep. Eggs are laid on the trunks of poplars and willows, and pass winter in this state, hatching the following spring. Caterpillars cling close to twigs, camouflaged against the bark. Found in woodland, especially in damp areas.

Svensson's Copper Underwing ▪ *Amphipyra berbera* 5cm (wingspan)

DESCRIPTION Sturdy, thick-bodied moth. Forewings dark brown, with obscure paler band running across about two-thirds the way down, otherwise finely vermiculated, spotted and scalloped. Underwings uniform rich, warm copper-orange without dark border. Egg round, ridged. Caterpillar plump, tapering towards head; green with dark-edged yellow line down sides, small horn at tail end. Pupa brown, formed underground. The very similar **Copper Underwing** *A. pyramidea* has paler palps on head.

DISTRIBUTION Widespread in Europe, but not reaching N Sweden or Scotland.
HABITS AND HABITAT Nocturnal, flying Jul–Sep. Overwinters as an egg on a foodplant – any of various deciduous woody plants, including Common Hawthorn (p. 113), Blackthorn *Prunus spinosa* and oaks. Hatches in spring, descending the tree to pupate in the soil in midsummer. Woodland, scrubland, parks and gardens.

Blotched Emerald

■ *Comibaena bajularia* 2.5cm (wingspan)

DESCRIPTION Attractive green moth, one of several similar species. Wings bright, cold green with scalloped black and white borders and 2 fine white lines running across. Pale blotches on inside corners of both fore- and hindwings. Body slender, not very hairy. Egg round, greyish, glossy. Caterpillar a brown looper; attaches fragments of vegetation to its body for camouflage. Pupa light brown, formed inside a cocoon in leaf litter.

DISTRIBUTION Quite common across Europe, but not reaching Scotland and only in S in Sweden.

HABITS AND HABITAT Flies at night in May–Jun, attracted to light (especially males). Eggs are laid on leaves of oak trees, and the caterpillar hibernates while still small, resuming feeding the following spring. Woodlands with good numbers of mature Pedunculate Oaks (p. 110) or Sessile Oaks *Quercus petraea*.

Straw Dot

■ *Rivula sericealis* 2cm (wingspan)

DESCRIPTION Delicate, pale moth. Wings held at 45 degrees to body. Pale straw-brown, shading to darker red-brown at wing edge, with dark brown diffuse spot in centre of forewing. Underwings whitish. Slender body, legs and antennae. Palps project forwards, giving it a 'snouted' appearance. Caterpillar green with double white line either side of back, and sparse but obvious longish, dark hairs; tapers towards tail end. Pupa green, formed among grasses.

DISTRIBUTION Common across most of Europe, becoming scarcer further N.

HABITS AND HABITAT Nocturnal, attracted to light. Is thought to be a recent colonist of the UK. 2 generations fly each year, in Jun–Jul and again in Aug–Sep. Eggs are laid on grasses, and the caterpillar pupates among grass leaves. Damp woodland and meadows.

Green Carpet
■ *Colostygia pectinataria* 2.5cm (wingspan)

DESCRIPTION Attractive, delicate, small, triangular-shaped moth. Wings mossy green, with light and dark bands and scalloping, forming a vague darker band midway down the forewings. Green colour fades to yellowish within a few days of emerging, when it becomes more difficult to separate from other related species. Hindwings pale, shading slightly darker towards edge. Egg round, reddish. Caterpillar red-brown, becoming greyer as it matures; large-headed. Pupa formed in loose soil.
DISTRIBUTION Widespread and common across Europe.
HABITS AND HABITAT Nocturnal, flies May–Jul. Occasionally produces a 2nd generation in late summer in S areas. Eggs are laid on bedstraws and sometimes other plants, including Stinging Nettles (p. 117) and dead-nettles. Overwinters as a caterpillar. Found in a wide variety of habitats, including woodland, moorland and heathland.

Garden Carpet
■ *Xanthorhoe fluctuata* 2cm (wingspan)

DESCRIPTION Small greyish moth. Holds wings at 45 degrees to body, giving it a triangular shape. Forewings mainly mottled and finely banded mid-grey, with blackish patches on 'shoulders' close to body (thorax and head also blackish, and broad, dark band midway down, darkest at outside edge). Hindwings whitish, becoming slightly darker towards edge. Body and legs relatively slender and delicate. Caterpillar a greenish or dark green looper, twig-like in shape. Pupates underground.
DISTRIBUTION Common and widespread across Europe.
HABITS AND HABITAT Nocturnal; attracted to light, and often found resting on walls near outside lights. Breeds continuously through summer, so may be seen anytime from Apr to Sep. Eggs laid on cabbages, nasturtiums and other related plants. Winter is spent in the pupal stage. Found in gardens, allotments, parks and many other habitats.

Silver Ground Carpet
■ *Xanthorhoe montanata* 2.5cm (wingspan)

DESCRIPTION Pale silvery moth with dark patterning, showing typical triangular carpet moth shape at rest. Similar to Garden Carpet (p. 78) in pattern, rather variable but always has pale silver-white ground colour. Dark central band across forewings usually more obvious than dark 'shoulders', and thorax paler, so lacks the 'dark-fronted' look of Garden Carpet. Caterpillar a twig-like looper. Pupa formed in a cocoon, buried in loose earth.
DISTRIBUTION Common and widespread across Europe.
HABITS AND HABITAT Nocturnal, though is sometimes seen flying by day. Adults emerge in May and may be seen into Jul; they are regularly attracted to light. Foodplants include a variety of low-growing species such as bedstraws, violets and primroses. Overwinters in the larval stage, pupating underground in spring. Found in a variety of habitats, including woodland, sheltered scrubland, wetlands and gardens.

Barred Yellow
■ *Cidaria fulvata* 2cm (wingspan)

DESCRIPTION Attractive carpet moth, with the group's typical triangular shape at rest. Forewings rich, warm yellow-orange, with narrow, dark band close to thorax and broader, darker band below that; outer edges also becoming darker but with pale triangular wedge at wing-tip. Underwings creamy white. Caterpillar a green looper with yellow stripe down side. Pupa formed in loose soil.
DISTRIBUTION Widespread but sometimes patchily distributed across most of Europe, becoming scarcer further N.
HABITS AND HABITAT Adults fly by night in Jun and Jul. Foodplants are roses, both native wild species and cultivated varieties. Overwinters as an egg, hatching in spring. The caterpillar feeds throughout spring, coming down from the foodplant to pupate in late May. Found in gardens, parks, scrubland and sheltered wooded areas.

Blood-vein ■ *Timandra comae* 2.5cm (wingspan)

DESCRIPTION Distinctive small moth. Ground colour yellowish grey, with pinkish-red borders to all wings and a red line running from tip of forewing to halfway up inner edge; a similar narrow red band across hindwings forms a continuous line in typical resting posture with wings almost fully open. All wing-tips come to a small hooked point. Caterpillar a grey-brown twig-like looper. Pupa light brown, formed among leaf litter.

DISTRIBUTION Common and widespread across much of Europe, but becoming scarcer further N and absent in far N.

HABITS AND HABITAT Adults fly by night in 2 generations, so may be seen anytime from May to Sep. Eggs are laid on various low-growing herbaceous plants, especially docks. The species overwinters as a caterpillar. Found in most sheltered, well-vegetated habitats, including woodlands and gardens.

Magpie Moth
■ *Abraxas grossulariata* 3.5cm (wingspan)

DESCRIPTION Striking moth with broad, round, butterfly-like wings. Wings white (occasionally yellow) with numerous black spots, forming a broad band across middle of forewings (narrower central band across hindwings) and also along borders and in patches close to body. Forewing central band and 'shoulders' also have some orange suffusion. Egg oval, whitish. Caterpillar greyish, becoming white with scattered black spots and diffuse orange side-stripe. Pupa banded black and yellow, attached by silk to a leaf.

DISTRIBUTION Common across much of Europe, becoming scarcer and more scattered further N.

HABITS AND HABITAT Flies by day and night in Jul and Aug, coming to light at night. Eggs are laid in clusters on leaves of currants, Common Hawthorn (p. 113) and sometimes other plants. Overwinters as a small caterpillar. Gardens, allotments and scrubby areas.

Canary-shouldered Thorn

■ *Ennomos alniaria* 4cm (wingspan)

DESCRIPTION Striking, stocky moth. Head, thorax and base of forewings covered in bright yellow hair. Wings otherwise brown with dark bands, uneven at edges. Often rests with wings partly open and raised above back (as do other thorn moths). Egg oblong, whitish. Caterpillar a slender looper, dark greyish with a broad, light green stripe down sides, becoming more evenly coloured as it matures. Pupa pale yellowish, formed among leaf litter.

DISTRIBUTION Common and widespread across Europe; scarcer in N Scandinavia.

HABITS AND HABITAT Adults are nocturnal, flying in 1 generation per year from Jul to Oct. They are attracted to light. Eggs are laid on various species of deciduous trees and winter is passed in this state – caterpillars hatch the following spring. Gardens, parks and woodlands.

Brimstone Moth

■ *Opisthograptis luteolata*
3.5cm (wingspan)

DESCRIPTION Distinctive delicate yellow moth. Normally rests with wings partly spread, sometimes raised above back. Wings light yellow, rather transparent, with brown marking and black-edged circle midway down outside edge of forewings and brown patch on forewing tip; border chequered brown. Head and body also light yellow. Egg oval, smooth, pale green. Caterpillar a brown or green looper, becoming greyer and more twig-like as it matures. Pupa brownish yellow, formed among leaf litter.

DISTRIBUTION Common and widespread across Europe, except the far N.

HABITS AND HABITAT Nocturnal, though sometimes seen flying by day. Has 1–3 generations a year depending on latitude – in most areas can be seen anytime between Apr and Sep. May overwinter as a part-grown caterpillar or pupa. Foodplants include Apple *Malus domestica*, birches and Bramble (p. 125). Gardens, parks and woodland.

Swallowtailed Moth
■ *Ourapteryx sambucaria* 4.5cm (wingspan)

DESCRIPTION Attractive and distinctive butterfly-like moth. Wings light yellow, rather transparent. 2 fine brown lines on forewings and 1 on hindwings (forming continuous line with inner forewing line when wings are open); all wings also have fine brown borders. Hindwings have short, pointed projections on outer corner. Egg round, ridged, yellow. Caterpillar a very slender, dull green or grey looper. Pupa formed within a cocoon on the foodplant.
DISTRIBUTION Common and widespread across most of Europe, but not reaching the far N of Scotland or northwards of S Sweden.
HABITS AND HABITAT Nocturnal, adults coming to light. Flies in Jul and early Aug. Eggs are laid on a variety of plants, including Common Hawthorn (p. 113), Ivy (p. 117), Blackthorn *Prunus spinosa* and Common Privet (p. 115). Overwinters as a caterpillar, concealed in bark. Gardens, woods and parkland.

Scorched Wing
■ *Plagodis dolabraria* 3cm (wingspan)

DESCRIPTION Pale moth with long, oval wings. Ground colour pale straw-brown, marked with close broken, uneven dark lines following oval shape of wing. Vague broad, darker bands at one-third and two-thirds points on forewings. Inner corners of all wings gradually darken to blackish brown, like burnt paper. Egg smooth, oval, pinkish. Caterpillar greenish, becoming dark grey when mature; loops. Pupa glossy red-brown, formed inside cocoon on the ground.
DISTRIBUTION Common across most of Europe; more scattered in Ireland and Scotland, and absent from N Sweden.
HABITS AND HABITAT Nocturnal – males are attracted to light but females are not. Adults fly May–Jun. Eggs are laid on oaks, birches, willows and other deciduous trees. Passes winter as a pupa, formed within leaf litter. Parks, gardens and woodland.

Winter Moth

■ *Operophtera brumata*
2.5cm (wingspan)

DESCRIPTION Rather undistinguished grey-brown moth. Male has full-sized light greyish-brown wings with subtle markings; long-legged. Female has tiny stumps of wings and does not fly; large, plump hairy abdomen. Egg blue, becoming brown as it develops. Caterpillar a green looper with yellow bands and side-stripe. Pupa red-brown, formed inside thick cocoon on the ground or just under soil surface. DISTRIBUTION Widespread and common throughout Europe. HABITS AND HABITAT Nocturnal. Flying season begins in late autumn and extends throughout winter. Eggs are laid on various deciduous trees, including oaks and Apple *Malus domestica*. Can be serious pest in Apple orchards. Pupates on the ground, from where the wingless females climb up into the trees, releasing pheromones to attract males. Gardens, orchards and woodlands.

December Moth

■ *Poecilocampa populi* 4cm (wingspan)

DESCRIPTION Dark, rather furry moth. Wings rather translucent against the light; dark brown, with whitish band across wing bases (and thorax) and another at about the two-thirds point; wing edges shade to paler brown; hindwings lighter. Body plump and furry. Male smaller than female, with feathery antennae. Egg oval, speckled dark and pale. Caterpillar dull pale greenish brown, fairly hairy, tapering at both ends. Pupa squat, blackish, formed in cracks in bark. DISTRIBUTION Common and widespread across Europe. HABITS AND HABITAT Nocturnal. Flies from late autumn into winter. Eggs are laid on the twigs of a foodplant tree, and pass the winter in this state. Foodplants are a wide variety of deciduous trees, including alders, birches, Ash *Fraxinus excelsior*, poplars, oaks and willows. Woodland, parks, gardens and other habitats where suitable trees grow.

Mottled Umber
■ *Erannis defoliaria* 3.5cm (wingspan)

DESCRIPTION Only the male has wings; female is completely wingless. Male coloration variable, usually warm mid-brown with broad, darker bands across forewings at one-third and two-thirds points. Ground colour can be much paler, and banding much less strongly contrasting. Female leggy, plump, pale yellowish with heavy dark spotting, and legs alternately banded pale and dark. Egg oval, pale. Caterpillar a greyish or brownish looper, with dark and light side-stripes. Pupa glossy red-brown.
DISTRIBUTION Widespread and common across most of Europe, but scare and becoming absent in the far N.
HABITS AND HABITAT Nocturnal. Emerges late in the year and may be seen between Oct and Dec. Foodplants include various deciduous trees; as with other wingless female moths, the female climbs strongly among the tree twigs. Males locate females by scent. Gardens, parks and woodland.

Peppered Moth
■ *Biston betularia* 5cm (wingspan)

DESCRIPTION Long-winged moth. Wings and body are evenly and finely speckled with black and white, appearing grey at any distance. Dark form with few or no white speckles sometimes seen, especially in urban areas. Male antennae very feathery. Egg oval, shiny. Caterpillar a twig-like looper, green or brown. Pupa glossy, squat, blackish, formed underground.
DISTRIBUTION Common across most of Europe, but not present in far N.
HABITS AND HABITAT Nocturnal. Adults fly in May and Jun. Foodplants include assorted deciduous trees. Mature caterpillars pupate in late autumn, with adults emerging in the spring. The species became famous as a living example of natural selection when the normally rare dark form prospered in industrialised towns in the 1950s, camouflaged against sooty walls and tree trunks. Most habitats.

Mottled Beauty
■ *Alcis repandata* 4cm (wingspan)

DESCRIPTION Variable grey moth. Rests with wings spread. Delicately patterned with fine wavering bands, scalloping, speckles and spots. Some individuals show a more contrasting pattern, sometimes including broad, solid, dark bands across middle of forewings. Always shows a dark, curved line across 'shoulders'. Egg oval. Caterpillar a twig-like looper, varying in colour from red-brown to greenish or grey. Pupa formed in soil.
DISTRIBUTION Common and widespread across most of Europe, numbers thinning out further N.
HABITS AND HABITAT Nocturnal, strongly attracted to light. Adults are on the wing in Jun and Jul. Eggs are laid on a variety of woody plants, and the caterpillar overwinters on a plant stem while still small, completing its development and pupating the following spring. Gardens, woods, heathland and parkland.

Broad-bodied Chaser
■ *Libellula depressa* 7cm (wingspan)

Female

DESCRIPTION A sturdy dragonfly. Body broad and short, rather flattened and blunt-tipped (especially in female). In male, head and thorax dark blackish brown, abdomen powder-blue with small black tip. All body parts greenish brown in female. Both have row of yellow patches down sides. Wings clear, darker at base (hindwings have dark triangular patch); dark spots on tip on leading edge. Nymph aquatic, short-bodied and long-legged, wingless, blackish brown.
DISTRIBUTION Common throughout much of Europe, absent from Scotland, Ireland and north Sweden.
HABITS AND HABITAT On the wing from May through to the end of summer. Nymph catches prey underwater; adult hunts other flying insects. Adults frequently rest on prominent perches with wings pushed forwards, and are aggressively territorial. Pairs form 'wheel' shape when copulating. Female dips abdomen tip in water to lay eggs. Found near still water.

Female

Speckled Bush-cricket
■ *Leptophyes punctatissima* 1.5cm (length)

DESCRIPTION Green grasshopper-like insect with very long, fine antennae. Mid-moss-green, very finely speckled all over with dark brown; usually also has a broad brown stripe running down back when fully mature. Fine white line runs through eye and onto sides of thorax. All legs long, especially hind pair, which flex up well clear of body. Flightless, small vestigial wings in male only. Female has short, claw-shaped ovipositor at rear. Earlier stages very similar to mature adult, and often show a yellow line down back.

DISTRIBUTION Widespread across much of Europe, including S Scandinavia.
HABITS AND HABITAT Usually keeps out of sight within plants. Mostly vegetarian. Eggs are laid in plant stems or tree bark, hatching the following spring. Adults are mature by late summer. Song is a soft chirp. Hedgerows, gardens and woodland.

Female

Oak Bush-cricket
■ *Meconema thalassinum* 1.5cm (length)

DESCRIPTION Light grass-green bush-cricket, with extremely long, fine antennae. Pale line down back from head to abdomen tip. Hind legs long and powerful. Thorax has brown smudges on sides. Wings on mature adult long, reaching abdomen tip when at rest (though not beyond ovipositor in female). Ovipositor long and scimitar-shaped with an upward curve. Earlier stages wingless, otherwise similar to adult.

DISTRIBUTION Common across much of Europe, reaching S Sweden but not Scotland.
HABITS AND HABITAT Usually found in oak trees. Flies well when mature and is attracted to light. Feeds primarily on aphids and other small prey; also eats leaves. Eggs are laid in bark cracks, hatching the following May. Adults mature by midsummer and survive into Oct. 'Song' is a quiet drumming. Found wherever oaks grow.

Dark Bush-cricket
■ *Pholidoptera griseoaptera* 2cm (length)

DESCRIPTION Dark grey-green
(sometimes paler or reddish) bush-cricket
with very long antennae and long, spindly
hind legs; rather heavy-bodied and squat.
Underside yellow or greenish yellow.
Female lacks wings; male wings tiny
and non-functional. Early stages have
pronounced dark-bordered orange-yellow
line down back from head to abdomen
tip. Female ovipositor is long with a
strong upward curve.

DISTRIBUTION Common across much
of Europe, but not reaching Scotland or
beyond central Sweden.

HABITS AND HABITAT Lives among
leaves in thick vegetation, feeding on plant matter and small insects. Eggs are laid in bark
cracks or rotting wood, hatching the following spring. Nymphs mature by midsummer.
Mature males produce a churring 'song' at dusk to attract females and deter rival males,
this continuing into mid-autumn. Found in all sheltered, well-vegetated habitats.

Common Froghopper
■ *Philaenus spumarius* 8mm (length)

DESCRIPTION Small but quite long-legged member
of the 'true bugs' (order Hemiptera). Body short and
smoothly oval but tapering to a point at tail end;
wings held in tent shape over back. Head flattened,
frog-like. Adult coloration quite variable, usually
brownish or blackish with more or less extensive
white patches on sides. In early stages is bright
yellow or green, and lives in a blob of froth
('cuckoo spit') as protection against predators.

DISTRIBUTION Common and widespread
across Europe.

HABITS AND HABITAT Lives in low herbaceous
vegetation, sucking plant sap with its specialised
mouthparts. Adults spring very rapidly and
powerfully from plant to plant. Nymphs lack adults'
camouflage and jumping ability, so secrete a blob of
foam to shelter themselves as they feed and mature.
Meadows, hedgerows and similar habitats.

Hawthorn Shield Bug

■ *Acanthosoma haemorrhoidale* 1.6cm (length)

DESCRIPTION Broad-bodied, shield-shaped 'true bug', widest just behind head. Long antennae, and fairly long legs and wings that fit tightly to body. Head pointed, 'shoulders' rising steeply when viewed from side. Mature adults brown with green sides, legs and underside. Also has triangular green patch just behind 'shoulders'. Nymphs green all over, wingless and more rounded, lacking the adults' square 'shoulders'.

DISTRIBUTION Common across most of Europe, and has expanded its range northwards in recent decades.

HABITS AND HABITAT Usually found on Common Hawthorn (p. 113) but sometimes on other plants. Feeds on sap sucked from the berries or leaves. Hibernates in fully developed adult state, breeding the following spring. The young bugs pass through several moults, becoming progressively more adult-like until they mature in late summer. Scrubland and parks.

Bronze Shield Bug ■ *Eysarcoris fabricii* 7mm (length)

DESCRIPTION Small shield bug, rounder in shape than most and with less pronounced 'shoulders'. Adult grey-brown, with dark triangular marking at top of abdomen, and body

edges clearly chequered black and white. Head dark, antennae banded dark and light, legs dark. Newly hatched nymphs are very round-bodied, red-brown with dark head and thorax, becoming more adult-like with each successive moult.

DISTRIBUTION Found across much of Europe, becoming scarcer and more scattered further N.

HABITS AND HABITAT Also known as the Woundwort Shield Bug, as woundworts are the preferred foodplants, although others such as dead-nettles may be used. Feeds on plant sap, folding their sucking mouthparts under the head when not in use. Early-stage nymphs live in close colonies; adults may also be found in groups. Hedgerows and other well-vegetated habitats.

Blackfly ▪ *Aphis fabae* 3mm (length)

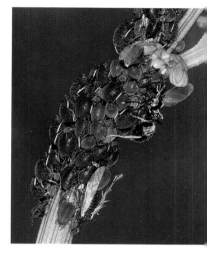

DESCRIPTION Tiny black aphid, also known as Black Bean Aphid, which may be winged or wingless. Small head with relatively long antennae, small thorax and large, plump abdomen. Legs rather long and yellowish with black feet. Winged adults have 2 pairs of narrow, clear wings, held tent-like when at rest. Forewings considerably larger than hindwings.

DISTRIBUTION Common and widespread across Europe.

HABITS AND HABITAT Feeds by sucking sap from a wide variety of plants, and secretes honeydew. Females give birth to genetic clones without needing to mate (parthenogenesis), and so dense colonies soon form, carpeting plant stems. In late summer, females produce winged males and females, which fly off to mate and lay eggs, these overwintering. Gardens and other well-vegetated habitats.

Rose Aphid
▪ *Macrosiphum rosae*
4mm (length)

DESCRIPTION Also known as Greenfly. Small reddish or greenish aphid, which may be seen with or without wings. Long legs blackish at joints, long antennae blackish at base. Young nymphs essentially the same as adults but smaller – colonies often have individuals of a variety of sizes.

DISTRIBUTION Common across Europe.

HABITS AND HABITAT Lives and feeds on rose bushes, both wild and cultivated varieties, and forms very dense colonies where not controlled with insecticides. Later in summer may colonise plants of other species. Females produce live wingless young and, later in the year or when the colony becomes overcrowded, winged young of both sexes that are capable of conventional sexual reproduction. These migrate to new sites, mate and lay eggs, which overwinter. Parks, gardens and hedgerows.

Green Lacewing
■ *Chrysoperla carnea* 3cm (wingspan)

DESCRIPTION Bright green flying insect. Has 2 pairs of large wings, clear but with a dense network of bright green veins, so the effect is of shimmering green lace – hence its common name. Body visible through wings when at rest. Head, thorax and abdomen bright green. Antennae long, legs rather short. Face delicately pointed; eyes reddish, glowing in artificial light. Larva wingless with flattened, bristly brownish-yellow body, short antennae and very large jaws. Pupates in white silk cocoon in a dead leaf.

DISTRIBUTION Widespread and common across Europe.

HABITS AND HABITAT Predatory insect that flies mainly at night, attracted to light. Preys predominantly on aphids (as do the wingless larvae); adults may also drink flower nectar. It hibernates in its adult form, producing a midsummer generation the following year. Gardens, parks and woods.

Female

Common Earwig
■ *Forficula auricularia* 1.3cm (length)

DESCRIPTION Fast-running, dark brown beetle-like insect with a pair of short wings folded away under small wingcases, not covering the long, segmented abdomen. Has large eyes and a narrow neck. Has large pincers at abdomen tip (used when mating) – curved inwards in males, smaller and straighter in females. Long antennae. Wings rounded, clear and shiny. Egg white, shiny, oval. Nymph is a shorter, squatter version of adult, with full-sized pincers but lacking wings.

DISTRIBUTION Common and widespread across most of Europe, reaching central Sweden.

HABITS AND HABITAT Nocturnal, often living among leaf litter and sheltering in rotting wood. Overwinters as an adult. Sometimes enters houses. Feeds on plant matter. Female lays eggs in underground burrow and brings food for the young nymphs for the first few days of their lives.

Scorpionfly ■ *Panorpa communis*
3cm (wingspan)

DESCRIPTION 4-winged flying insect with a distinctive shape. Has long antennae and a long, downward-pointing 'beak'. Abdomen dark with light bands, orange-red at tip. Female's abdomen tapers to a point, but in male it has a swollen bulb like a scorpion's sting. Wings large, narrow and oval, clear with dark broken bands across and dark tips. Larva light grey-brown, resembling a slightly bristly caterpillar. Pupa formed in a silk-lined chamber underground. DISTRIBUTION Widespread across most of Europe, commoner in the S. HABITS AND HABITAT Flies with reluctance, and usually seen resting among shady vegetation. Adults are active through

Male

summer. Feeds mainly by scavenging dead insects and also eating fruit. Eggs are laid on the ground, and the larva remains there, feeding mainly on dead insects before pupating underground over the winter. Shady, well-vegetated, low-lying habitats.

Cranefly ■ *Tipula paludosa* 2cm (length)

DESCRIPTION 'True fly' with 1 pair of long, narrow wings. All legs extremely long. Head small with projecting, beak-like mouthparts; antennae quite short. Thorax small. Abdomen long and slender, with a slight bulge before the pointed tip (bulge more pronounced in females that are about to lay eggs). Larvae ('leatherjackets') are brown, tough-skinned, long-bodied and legless, and live underground. DISTRIBUTION Common and widespread throughout N Europe. HABITS AND HABITAT Adults emerge from summer but are commonest in autumn, sometimes swarming across open grassland. They feed very little, if at all. Eggs are laid on the ground, and the larvae live in the soil, feeding on the roots of grasses. Overwinters as a larva, pupating near the soil surface. Open grassland, lawns, heaths and parkland; often enters buildings.

Sunfly ▪ *Helophilus pendulus*
1.4cm (length)

DESCRIPTION Large, broad-bodied and boldly pattered hoverfly, yellow and black to mimic a wasp. Head yellow with black eyes. Antennae very short. Thorax black with 4 narrow yellow lines down its length. Abdomen yellow with broad black bands across – top 2 bands connected with a small black stripe. 1 pair of clear wings. Larva develops in water and is a legless grub with a long, fine breathing tube (a 'rat-tailed maggot').
DISTRIBUTION Common across N Europe, extending into the far N.
HABITS AND HABITAT Often found near still water. Eggs are laid in water – ditches, ponds, rivers and even sometimes small puddles. Adults fly from Apr to Oct, feeding on flower nectar and basking on vegetation. Usually found near water.

Common Banded Hoverfly ▪ *Syrphus ribesii* 1.3cm (length)

DESCRIPTION Dainty hoverfly, patterned to resemble a wasp. Head dominated by large reddish eyes. Antennae very short. Thorax brownish, slightly furry. Abdomen black with yellow bands across, top band broken by narrow black bridge to form 2 yellow patches rather than a complete band. Wings clear with dark brown veins. Larva greyish, rather long-bodied, legless, resembling a slug.
DISTRIBUTION Common and widespread across Europe.
HABITS AND HABITAT Adults are on the wing from May to Nov. They feed on flower nectar and aphid honeydew. In common with other hoverflies, they have no sting, although they resemble wasps. They often hover on the spot for several seconds at a time, before making rapid course changes. The larvae are voracious predators of aphids. Gardens, parks, hedgerows and woodlands.

Greenbottle

■ *Lucilia caesar* 1cm (length)

DESCRIPTION Short-bodied, 2-winged 'true fly'; one of several similar species. Eyes large, reddish; antennae very short. Thorax and abdomen iridescent bright green, becoming bronze with age. Bristly hairs on body and longish legs. Wings clear, long, triangular-shaped, broadest at midpoint. Egg yellow. Larva a yellowish-white legless maggot. Pupa also pale, more squat and with pointed tip. DISTRIBUTION Common and widespread across Europe. HABITS AND HABITAT As this species may overwinter as a mature larva, a pupa or an adult, adults may be seen on the wing at any time. They lay numerous eggs on carrion, and sometimes even in wounds on still-living animals. The maggots consume the decaying flesh, leave the corpse and pupate in the ground. Found in most habitats, but rarely seen in buildings.

Flesh Fly ■ *Sarcophaga carnaria* 1.5cm (length)

DESCRIPTION Large, 2-winged fly. Several related species look very similar. Thorax black with white longitudinal stripes, abdomen chequered black and white. Body and legs bristly; has large round pads on feet. Eyes red. Wings clear, oval. Larva a white legless maggot; pupa similar. DISTRIBUTION Common and widespread across Europe. HABITS AND HABITAT Adults may be seen on the wing at any time of year. They feed on nectar, as well as carrion and dung. The eggs develop and hatch while still within the female's body, so live larvae are deposited onto the animal corpse on which they will feed. Sometimes enters buildings if attracted by the smell of food. Mature larvae crawl away from the corpse and pupate within the soil. Found in all kinds of habitats, especially farmland.

Common House-fly
■ *Musca domestica* 8mm (length)

DESCRIPTION Small, dull-coloured fly. Head and thorax grey-brown, eyes reddish and antennae short. Thorax marked with vague longitudinal stripes. Body and legs covered with short, dark bristles. Abdomen dull yellowish, with a dark stripe down back. Wings clear, usually folded across back. Egg white, long. Larva a white legless maggot, tapering towards head. Pupa brown, its colour darkening as it matures.
DISTRIBUTION Common and widespread throughout Europe.
HABITS AND HABITAT May be seen flying by day at any time of year. Adults feed on a wide variety of substances. Eggs are laid on all kinds of organic matter, including uncovered foodstuffs in homes. Maggots pupate close to food sources. The species can reproduce continuously, taking 10 days to complete its life cycle. Occurs in and around houses.

Bluebottle
■ *Calliphora erythrocephala* 1.1cm (length)

DESCRIPTION Fairly large, dark fly – one of several closely related and very similar-looking species. Head, abdomen and thorax blackish, with glossy blue sheen on abdomen. Eyes dull red. Antennae small. Wings clear, held partly open across back. Legs and body covered in bristles. Produces a loud buzzing in flight. Egg elongated, whitish. Larva a pale, legless maggot. Pupa darker, a squat cylinder.
DISTRIBUTION Common and widespread across Europe.
HABITS AND HABITAT Flies in the daytime, and may be seen at any time of year. Adults feed on a variety of foodstuffs, including flower nectar. Eggs are laid on decaying dead animals or other organic matter, hatching within hours. Maggots feed for a few days, then pupate for a few days more. Most often seen close to or inside houses.

Black Garden Ant
■ *Lasius niger* 5mm (length)

DESCRIPTION Most familiar garden ant species. Entirely dull black. Worker ants are wingless. Head, thorax and abdomen well defined, with narrow joins. Legs and antennae relatively long. Eyes small, jaws quite large. Queens considerably larger than workers, and males somewhat larger; males and newly emerged queens have 2 pairs of clear wings. Egg white. Larva white, legless, clearly segmented and rather squat, tapering at tail end. Pupa formed in yellowish-white cocoon.

DISTRIBUTION Found all over Europe.
HABITS AND HABITAT Nests underground, often beneath a stone. Colonies usually have a single queen, which lays eggs, while the sexually inactive workers maintain the colony, forage for food (omnivorous) for the larvae, and defend the site from predators. Winged males and new queens emerge in summer to mate. Gardens.

Red Ant
■ *Myrmica rubra* 6mm (length)

DESCRIPTION Similar in shape to Black Garden Ant (above), but slightly larger, with relatively longer legs and antennae. Coloration red all over, darkening a little on the head and abdomen tip. Males and newly emerged queens are winged; after mating, queens lose their wings but are clearly larger than the workers. Eggs, larva and pupa similar to those of Black Garden Ant.
DISTRIBUTION Common and widespread throughout Europe.
HABITS AND HABITAT Forms an

underground nest, which holds multiple queens. Workers collect food for the colony, which includes honeydew 'milked' from aphids, as well as plant and animal matter. Aggressive; can give a painful sting. Males and new winged queens emerge to mate in summer. Males then die, and the queens shed their wings and found new colonies. Gardens, woodlands and many other vegetated habitats.

Hornet ■ *Vespa crabro* 3.2cm (length)

DESCRIPTION Very large wasp. Body sections divided by narrow joins. Face yellow when viewed head-on, with large, dark eyes and long, sturdy antennae. Top of head and thorax brown, abdomen yellow with brown bands at each segment join. 2 pairs of narrow wings, these hooking together in flight to give the impression of a single pair. Early stages not seen outside nest.

DISTRIBUTION Widespread but patchily distributed across Europe; absent from Scotland, Ireland and N Sweden.

HABITS AND HABITAT Social wasp. Queens hibernate, emerging in spring to create a papery chambered nest in a sheltered spot, such as within a hollow tree – they chew wood to produce the 'paper'. Workers feed on nectar and fruit, and bring insect prey to the nest. Males and new queens mate in summer. Woodlands.

German Wasp
■ *Vespula germanica*
2.2cm (length)

DESCRIPTION Black and yellow wasp, 1 of several similar species. Head black, face yellow with black markings between antennae and 3 small black dots between eyes. Eyes and antennae black. Thorax mainly black; legs yellow; abdomen yellow, banded and spotted with black. 2 pairs of narrow, clear wings. Early stages not seen outside nest.

DISTRIBUTION Common across much of Europe, but scarcer in far W and N.

HABITS AND HABITAT Social wasp, the queen building a football-like papery nest in a sheltered spot (sometimes in buildings). Life cycle similar to that of Hornet (*above*). Larvae are fed on a diet of aphids, caterpillars and other insects, and secrete a sweet honeydew that the workers eat; workers also feed on nectar, windfall fruit and other sweet substances. Found in all kinds of sheltered habitats.

Red-tailed Bumblebee
■ *Bombus lapidarius* 1.3cm (length)

DESCRIPTION Plump and very hairy bumblebee.
Broad head with short black antennae, black
eyes and legs. Abdomen black with red tip.
May show yellow pollen sacs on hind legs. Males
have a yellow band on thorax. 2 pairs of narrow,
clear wings. Early stages not seen outside the
nest. The cuckoo bee *Psithyrus rupestris* mimics
this species; it is very similar but less hairy,
so its abdomen segments are more visible.
DISTRIBUTION Quite widespread and common
across Europe, but not reaching the far N.
HABITS AND HABITAT A social bee, with
queens establishing colonies of some 150
individuals in an underground nest furnished with
wax cells. Workers collect nectar and pollen to
nourish the larvae, which pupate inside cocoons
when mature. Gardens and other flowery habitats.

Honey Bee
■ *Apis mellifera* 1.6cm (length)

DESCRIPTION Slimmer and less hairy
than bumblebees. Body sections clearly
separated by narrow joins. Head and
thorax black, covered with brown hair.
Eyes black; antennae fine and black.
Abdomen less hairy, banded black and
brown. Legs black, with yellow pollen
sacs often visible on hind legs. 2 pairs
of narrow wings, fixed together in flight
so they appear to be a single pair.
Early stages not seen outside nest.
DISTRIBUTION Widespread and
common across most of Europe.
HABITS AND HABITAT Colonial,
its nests containing tens of thousands
of workers and 1 queen. Kept
commercially but also exists in a wild
state, nesting in sheltered spots. Larvae
live and pupate within wax cells. Workers gather nectar and pollen.
Honey is stored as winter food for the colony. Found wherever flowers grow.

Ground Beetle
■ *Pterostichus madidus* 1.4cm (length)

DESCRIPTION Glossy black ground-dwelling beetle. Body sections clearly separated by narrow joins. Head rounded, with fairly long antennae and strong jaws. Thorax shield-shaped. Legs relatively long and sturdy, black (sometimes reddish close to base), with small barbs on end section. Abdomen oval, with fine longitudinal ridges on wingcases, so appears less glossy than head and thorax. Larva brown, blacker towards head; long-bodied and segmented, with 6 well-developed legs; powerful jaws.

DISTRIBUTION Common in W Europe; scarce and becoming absent further E and N.
HABITS AND HABITAT A predatory beetle. Hibernates as an adult and is active from spring, searching for insects and other invertebrate prey on the ground among leaf litter. The larva is also predatory, tackling slower-moving prey such as slugs. Well-vegetated habitats.

Violet Ground Beetle
■ *Carabus violaceus* 2.5cm (length)

DESCRIPTION Large black ground beetle with a violet sheen. Head bears strong jaws and long, sturdy, clearly segmented antennae. Thorax round, smooth, with 2 backward-pointing projections where it joins the abdomen, which is large and oval. Wingcases have very fine longitudinal ridges. Legs long, sturdy, clearly segmented. Larva light brown, darker at head end; long-bodied and clearly segmented, with 6 legs close to head end; strong jaws.
DISTRIBUTION Occurs throughout Europe.
HABITS AND HABITAT Seen mainly in summer. Active particularly at night, hunting on the ground. Often shelters under rocks. Females lay eggs on plants. Larvae dwell among leaf litter and are predatory like the adults. They pupate underground or in rotten wood, emerging in autumn and hibernating. Gardens and farmland.

Devil's Coach-horse

■ *Staphylinus olens* 2.5cm (length)

DESCRIPTION Long-bodied black
beetle with a dull sheen. Head,
thorax and abdomen are of even
thickness. Has relatively short antennae
and strong, curved jaws. Thorax about the
same size as head. Wingcases very short,
reaching a quarter way down abdomen;
exposed part of abdomen is clearly
segmented and flexible. Legs long and
strong. Larva very similar to adult but
coloration paler. Shiny brown pupa
formed in leaf litter.
DISTRIBUTION Common and widespread across Europe.
HABITS AND HABITAT A predatory beetle that seldom flies, instead hunting its prey
on the ground. Nocturnal, and may be seen Apr–Oct. When threatened, it raises its head,
opens its jaws and curls up its abdomen tip; it can also squirt foul-smelling fluid. Larvae
are also predatory, and live in leaf litter or topsoil. Hibernates as an adult. Woodlands,
parks and gardens.

Seven-spot Ladybird

■ *Coccinella 7-punctata* 6mm (length)

DESCRIPTION Round beetle with
distinctive patterning. Head and thorax
small, black with white spots; abdomen
round. Wingcases scarlet, glossy, with
3 symmetrical round spots on each, plus
another black mark at top inside edge
of each wingcase that forms the 7th spot
when wingcases are closed. Legs and
antennae shortish, black. Egg orange,
elongated. Larva long-bodied, bluish
black with small yellow spots and tufts
of black bristles. Pupa patterned like
larva but round.
DISTRIBUTION Common and
widespread across most of Europe.
HABITS AND HABITAT Active day and night, preying on aphids. Hibernates as an
adult in sheltered spots (sometimes in buildings). Flies strongly. Large numbers sometimes
migrate to the UK from Continental Europe. Eggs are laid on the undersides of leaves;
the larvae eat aphids. Gardens, hedgerows, woodlands and other well-vegetated habitats.

Two-spot Ladybird

■ *Adalia bipunctata* 4mm (length)

DESCRIPTION Small ladybird. Head and thorax black with white spots. Short black antennae and legs. Abdomen round, wingcases red or orange-red with 1 large black spot at centre of each. Colour variations are not unusual, including forms with red-spotted black wing cases, or more than 1 spot on each wingcase. Egg elongated. Larva grey, long-bodied, with a few orange spots, bristly tufts and 6 legs. Pupa shaped like adult, but yellowish, becoming darker as it matures. DISTRIBUTION Common and widespread throughout most of Europe. HABITS AND HABITAT As with other ladybirds, feeds on aphids in both larval and adult stages. The larvae are also cannibalistic. Adults hibernate in sheltered spots, frequently entering outbuildings. Found in gardens, woodland, hedgerows and other well-vegetated habitats.

Harlequin Ladybird

■ *Harmonia axyridis* 8mm (length)

DESCRIPTION Large, very variable ladybird. Head and thorax black and white, often showing more white than black. Antennae and legs shortish. Wingcases usually orange with numerous black spots of variable size; in some cases, the spots are very small, in others they combine to form blotches. Black variants with or without red or orange spots also occur. Larva mostly black, long-bodied and spiny, with variable orange speckles. Pupa round, variable in colour. DISTRIBUTION Originally from E Asia. Introduced to the UK and elsewhere in Europe, and rapidly expanding its range. HABITS AND HABITAT Like other ladybirds, this is a predator of aphids. Adults also feed on soft fruit in autumn when preparing to hibernate. Conservationists are concerned it is outcompeting native European ladybirds. Gardens, hedgerows and woodland.

Cockchafer
■ *Melolontha melolontha* 2.5cm (length)

DESCRIPTION Large, thickset beetle. Head and thorax blackish. Antennae brown, formed of 6 (females) or 7 (males) fanned 'leaves'. Thorax black, legs brown and sturdy. Abdomen broad, pointed at tip, banded dark and light when seen from below. Wingcases brown with well-spaced ridges. Larva a plump white grub with brown head and 6 very short legs. Pupa brownish, formed in soil.
DISTRIBUTION Occurs patchily across Europe.
HABITS AND HABITAT Nocturnal, strongly attracted to light and buzzes loudly in flight. Adults appear in May (hence its alternative common name of May Bug) and feed on deciduous tree foliage. Eggs are laid on soil; larvae dwell for 3 years underground, eating the roots of grasses, including cereals. Pupae hatch in autumn, with adults emerging the following spring. Farmland, parks and gardens.

Lily Beetle ■ *Lilioceris lilii* 1cm (length)

DESCRIPTION Distinctive red beetle. Head and thorax both small, abdomen much larger. Head black with large, protruding eyes and fairly long, clearly segmented antennae. Thorax orange-red, slightly spindle-shaped. Legs black, barbed on last joint. Abdomen much wider than thorax. Wingcases orange-red, square-cut along top edge and rounded at bottom. Egg red, becoming blacker; elongated. Larva rather short, greenish with black head, 6 small legs. Pupa formed in cocoon underground.
DISTRIBUTION Widespread and increasing its range across most of Europe; has recently begun to colonise Scotland.
HABITS AND HABITAT A herbivorous beetle, normally found on the leaves and flowers of lilies and related plants. Eggs are laid on leaf undersides, and larvae browse leaves and, later, flower heads, camouflaging themselves by carrying their own droppings on their backs. Gardens and parkland.

Vine Weevil

■ *Otiorhynchus sulcatus* 1cm (length)

DESCRIPTION Small, dull black beetle. Head and thorax lack obvious join; has small-headed and 'long-necked' appearance. Antennae long, relatively sturdy with kink at midpoint. Abdomen oval. Wingcases fused, covered in pitted longitudinal ridges. Legs sturdy, swollen at section nearest body and hooked at feet. Egg brown, tiny. Larva creamy white with brown head, slightly bristly; lacks visible legs. DISTRIBUTION Widespread across Europe. HABITS AND HABITAT Adults and larvae both consume a wide variety of plants, and can become a serious pest for gardeners. Adults are nocturnal, slowly clambering around on plants and feeding on leaf edges, leaving characteristic notched margins. Reproduces by parthenogenesis; eggs are laid on the ground, hatching into burrowing larvae that eat through roots and tubers. Gardens, parks, hedgerows and similar habitats.

Female

Garden Spider

■ *Araneus diadematus* 1.3cm (length)

DESCRIPTION Brown web-weaving spider. 8 fairly long, sturdy legs, these banded darker and lighter brown. Large abdomen, mottled in various shades of brown, with a vague whitish cross at centre. Mature females much larger than males. Egg yellow, found with others in large, round clumps attached to sheltered leaf or trunk. Newly hatched spiderling has yellow abdomen with dark patch. DISTRIBUTION Widespread and common across most of Europe. HABITS AND HABITAT Overwinters as an egg. Egg clusters hatch in spring and young spiders disperse by 'ballooning' – extruding a thread of silk and allowing the wind to carry them away. Females hang head-down in their large, round silk webs, these suspended between sturdy plants and with sticky threads to trap flying prey. Males scavenge from females' webs. Gardens, parks and hedgerows.

Common Cross Spider
■ *Araneus quadratus* 2cm (length)

DESCRIPTION Web-weaving spider. 8 sturdy legs, banded blackish and whitish. Abdomen very rounded and much larger than head in mature females ready to lay their eggs, about the same size as head in males; varies in colour from greenish to orange or rich brown, marked with a number of white spots, including 4 large central spots (clearest on dark-bodied individuals). Females much larger than males.
DISTRIBUTION Common and widespread across Europe.
HABITS AND HABITAT Builds a round web, usually much closer to the ground than that of the Garden Spider (p. 102) in order to catch jumping insects. The female's web includes a sheltered chamber by the side, used as a retreat during rain. Overwinters as an egg, hatching and dispersing the following spring. Gardens, woodlands, hedgerows and other well-vegetated habitats.

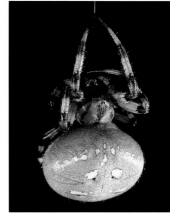

Female

House Spider ■ *Tegenaria domestica* 1cm (length)

DESCRIPTION Long-legged, long-bodied and powerfully built spider. Dull grey-brown and quite hairy all over, with a broad, paler stripe down back of cephalothorax. Abdomen oval, tapering at tip. Has large, gripping pedipalps with swollen tips on front of head. Males are relatively longer-legged, females relatively broader-bodied.
DISTRIBUTION Common and widespread across Europe.
HABITS AND HABITAT Adults may be seen year-round in sheltered places, including outbuildings. Often enters homes, although its presence is usually noticed and rarely tolerated. Builds a dense, flat sheet web, often across the corner of a room, with a funnel-shaped shelter within which it waits for prey to enter the web. Male shares female's web over several weeks, mating repeatedly, and is eaten by her when he dies. Gardens and buildings.

Female

Crab Spider

■ *Misumena vatia* 10cm (length)

DESCRIPTION Round-bodied spider that holds its long legs out sideways. Abdomen round and rather flattened, which together with the characteristic stance gives it a crab-like appearance. In female, abdomen is very rotund, much larger than cephalothorax, and colour is camouflaged to match surroundings – usually pure white, pure yellow or green. May have small double red spot or line on abdomen. Males much smaller than females and have brown stripes on slender, pale greenish abdomens. Eggs laid in a silk cocoon in a folded leaf.

DISTRIBUTION Found across much of Europe, but does not reach the far N.
HABITS AND HABITAT Does not spin a web, but lurks in white or yellow flowers to seize flying insects as they visit for nectar. Females change colour (gradually, over several days) to match their surroundings. Flowery habitats.

Common Woodlouse

■ *Oniscus asellus* 1.5cm (length)

DESCRIPTION Flattened, shiny grey ground-dwelling crustacean (related to shrimps, prawns and crabs), the most common of nearly 50 woodlouse species in the UK. Body oval, armoured and clearly segmented, with quite long, thick antennae and 7 pairs of legs (6 when first hatched). Body edges chequered with white in mature individuals. Newly hatched woodlice are pale but soon darken. DISTRIBUTION Common across much of Europe, but not reaching the far N. HABITS AND HABITAT Dwells in leaf litter, in decaying woodpiles, under stones and other damp-ground habitats. Feeds on various soft plant matter, as well as fungi. Can reproduce sexually and by parthenogenesis. The female carries eggs on the underside of her body for several weeks until they hatch. May live 4 years. Gardens, parks and many other sheltered habitats.

Pill Woodlouse

▪ *Armadillidium vulgare*
1.8cm (length)

DESCRIPTION Long-bodied, dark woodlouse. Usually greyish black, but may be reddish. Smoother at edges than Common Woodlouse (p. 104), and has scattering of pale speckles across segments. Is able to curl itself into a complete, tight ball, giving rise to popular alternative common name of Pill Bug. Long, back-curved antennae.

DISTRIBUTION Common across much of Europe, but does not reach the far N.

HABITS AND HABITAT As with other woodlice, forages for soft or decaying plant matter in damp, sheltered places on the ground. When threatened, it rolls into a ball, unlike Common Woodlouse, which plays dead. Moults its cuticle at regular intervals, starting at the tail end – newly moulted woodlice are pinkish. The old cuticle is usually eaten. Gardens, woodlands and other similar sheltered habitats.

Centipede

▪ *Lithobius variegatus* 3cm (length)

DESCRIPTION Many-legged, long-bodied animal. One of several similar species. Quite shiny, reddish brown. Head large, with long, often back-curved antennae. Number of body segments varies with age, but usually at least 7. Each segment bears a single pair of legs, banded with darker brown, the front pairs pointing forward, middle pairs at right angles to the body and rear pairs (which are the longest) swept backwards. Young centipedes are like shorter-bodied versions of adults.

DISTRIBUTION Found in the UK and parts of W mainland Europe.

HABITS AND HABITAT A predatory and fast-moving animal. Nocturnal, sheltering under stones and logs by day – it requires damp conditions. Hunts slower-moving ground animals such as woodlice and millipedes, disabling them with a venomous bite. Lacks eyes, so detects its prey by ground vibrations. Gardens, woodlands and parks.

Flat-backed Millipede ■ *Polydesmus angustus* 2.5cm (length)

DESCRIPTION Long-bodied, flattened, many-legged ground animal. Dull dark brown, mottled with paler colours, and with longish antennae. Usually has about 20 segments, each of which bears 2 pairs of side-projecting legs that are about half as long as the body is wide, becoming shorter at the tail end. In appearance, is much more centipede-like than most millipedes, which have a more tubular shape.
DISTRIBUTION Common and widespread across NW Europe.
HABITS AND HABITAT A herbivorous animal that dwells in leaf litter, compost heaps and other sheltered, damp places on the ground. It feeds mainly on decaying plant materials but also eats soft fruit. Females lay several batches of eggs following a mating. Hatchlings take up to 2 years to reach maturity and live much longer. Gardens and woodland.

Common Earthworm
■ *Lumbricus terrestris* 30cm (length)

DESCRIPTION Smooth, legless worm. Usually dull pinkish, shiny, darkening towards head end. Body clearly segmented, tapered at head end but blunt-ended at tail end. Fine bristles (to assist burrowing) visible on close examination. Small raised 'saddle' about one-third of the way from head. Young earthworms much smaller and more slender.
DISTRIBUTION Common and widespread across Europe.
HABITS AND HABITAT Lives underground, tunnelling almost 2m deep in the soil. Eats soil, digesting organic matter and excreting the rest into its tunnels near the surface, thereby restoring minerals to topsoil and improving soil fertility. Hermaphrodite. Comes to the surface to mate, exchanging egg and sperm cells, which unite outside the body in a cocoon. Surfaces after rain. Gardens and other habitats with soft soil.

Garden Snail

■ *Helix aspersa* 3.5cm (shell width)

DESCRIPTION Large, round-shelled snail. Shell coiled to form a bulge on 1 side; chequered light brown, usually with about 5 darker bands but sometimes evenly chequered dark and light. Body dull yellowish grey, soft, glistening, legless, loose and wrinkled along sides that touch the ground. 2 pairs of darker, bulb-tipped appendages at head end (top pair longer); tail end comes to a point. Eggs white, laid in clusters in soil indentations. Hatchlings have translucent shells.

DISTRIBUTION Common in the UK; more scattered in mainland NW Europe.

HABITS AND HABITAT Usually nocturnal, sheltering within the shell in the day. Eats a range of plant matter. Hermaphrodite – pairs exchange sperm following a prolonged courtship. Fertilisation occurs internally, and the snail digs shallow pits in soil in which to lay its eggs. Gardens.

Strawberry Snail

■ *Trichia striolata* 1.2cm (shell width)

DESCRIPTION Small, rather plain snail. Shell round from side, somewhat flattened in profile, tightly coiled and with more curls than that of Garden Snail (above). Mid- or dark brown with subtle paler mottling. Body dark, glistening greyish black, paler underneath; has similar shape and appendages to those of Garden Snail.

DISTRIBUTION Fairly common in the UK and mainland NW Europe, becoming rarer further E.

HABITS AND HABITAT Nocturnal, though may become active in wet conditions during the day. Feeds on plant matter; can become a pest of Strawberry *Fragaria* × *ananassa* patches. Like the Garden Snail, it is hermaphroditic; pairs fire a hormone-coated 'love dart' into each other's bodies prior to the prolonged copulation. Eggs are laid in the soil and the delicate hatchlings emerge a few weeks later. Found in gardens and allotments.

Large Red Slug ■ *Arion ater* 15cm (length)

DESCRIPTION Large, soft-bodied, legless ground animal. Body long, glistening, flat below and domed above, rather blunt-ended. Can contract into a rounded hump. May be reddish brown, brick-red, orange, grey or black (alternative name is Great Black Slug). Has smooth, round 'saddle' behind head containing breathing orifice; body otherwise with longitudinal ridges. Head bears 2 long and 2 short, bulbous-tipped appendages, longer pair above. Egg translucent, pearl-like.

DISTRIBUTION Common and widespread across most of Europe.

HABITS AND HABITAT Mainly nocturnal. Protects itself from drying out by secreting a layer of mucus, but does not venture far from damp, sheltered spots. Vegetarian, eating soft plant parts and fruit. Hermaphrodite. Eggs are laid in the autumn in loose soil, hatching the following spring. May live 3 years. Gardens and woodlands.

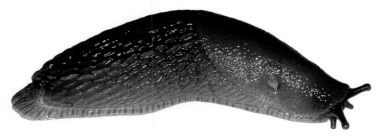

Common Garden Slug ■ *Arion distinctus* 3cm (length)

DESCRIPTION Small grey-brown slug. Long-bodied and blunt-ended. Head end darker, head appendages short and saddle rather indistinct; body has fine longitudinal ridges and vague yellowish stripe down back. Underside paler, yellowish orange. Egg round, translucent.

DISTRIBUTION Common and widespread across much of Europe.

HABITS AND HABITAT Herbivorous; very unpopular with gardeners as it can damage a wide range of plants. Mainly nocturnal, sheltering by day under stones or logs; requires damp environments. Hermaphrodite. Its courtship involves 1 partner following the other

in a circle, feeding on its mucus trail. Preyed upon by many birds and other animals – indiscriminate use of slug pellets is thought to be responsible for declines in some areas of species like Song Thrush (p. 25). Gardens, parkland, allotments, hedgerows and other sheltered, well-vegetated environments.

Leopard Slug
■ *Limax maximus* 20cm (length)

DESCRIPTION Very large slug. Long-bodied, tapering to a point at the tail end. Head appendages relatively long. Colour varies from yellowish to grey, with longitudinal dark bands or spots running down entire body. Some individuals look very strongly spotted, others are much less distinctly marked. Egg round, translucent.
DISTRIBUTION Occurs commonly throughout most of Europe.
HABITS AND HABITAT Feeds on plant matter, including rotting wood. Nocturnal, resting in a sheltered spot by day and often returning to the exact same nook after each night's wanderings. Hermaphrodite. Courting pairs climb a tree, then the entwined animals lower themselves on a thick thread of mucus before copulating. Both later lay hundreds of eggs in a sheltered place. Gardens, outbuildings, woods and other damp, sheltered habitats.

Silver Birch
■ *Betula pendula* 25m (height)

DESCRIPTION Elegant, usually rather slender deciduous tree. Trunk and branches have silver-white bark with fine darker flecks, streaks and larger dark fissures (bark red-brown in saplings). Foliage yellowish, often looks rather sparse and hanging. Leaves diamond- or triangle-shaped, up to 7cm long; margins have double row of teeth. Male catkins long, yellow, hanging, quite thick. Female catkins (on same tree) smaller, slimmer, erect, reddish or greenish. Mature female catkins break up into small windborne seeds.
DISTRIBUTION Widespread across most of Europe, especially in the N.
LIFE CYCLE AND HABITAT Lives for 80 years or more. Adaptable and tough, exploiting marginal environments in cold or exposed conditions, though is commonest on light, dry soils, such as heathlands and at the edges of coniferous forests.

Beech ■ *Fagus sylvatica* 30m (height)

DESCRIPTION Large, broad (where it has enough space), round-crowned deciduous tree. Foliage dense, spreading. Bark grey, fairly smooth and unmarked. Leaves oval and up to 15cm long; glossy with pronounced veins and slightly wavy margins; rather floppy; light green, becoming darker or (in 'Copper Beech' cultivar) reddish, purplish or black. Flowers in small, round clusters; male flowers hanging, female flowers erect. Fruit (beechmast) a pyramid-shaped brown nut, 2 or 3 developing in a woody case with bristly outer coating.

DISTRIBUTION Common across most of Europe, but becoming scarcer further N. Introduced to Scotland and Ireland.

LIFE CYCLE AND HABITAT Lives for more than 200 years. Found in lowland woodlands, where it may be the dominant species; also widely planted in parks and gardens. Very tolerant of shade.

Pedunculate Oak
■ *Quercus robur* 35m (height)

DESCRIPTION Usually broad, round-crowned deciduous tree. Foliage dense and spreading; branches long, gnarled and twisty, often reaching, or almost reaching, ground. Bark grey with many deep vertical fissures. Leaves up to 15cm long; yellowish, becoming dark green; short-stemmed, with up to 7 round-ended lobes on each side. Male flowers sparse, hanging green catkins; female flowers red, round, borne on long stems. Fruit an oval, glossy acorn in a pitted half-cup. Attacks by various insects lead to malformed acorns, and round galls on leaves and twigs.

DISTRIBUTION Common and widespread across most of Europe, extending as far N as central Sweden.

LIFE CYCLE AND HABITAT Lives for more than 500 years. Common in both lowland and upland woodlands, where it is often the dominant species and supports a huge diversity of animal life.

Horse Chestnut
▪ *Aesculus hippocastanum* 35m (height)

DESCRIPTION Tall, spreading deciduous tree, usually taller than it is broad. Round-crowned with dense foliage. Bark dark greyish and flaky, with shallow fissures both horizontally and vertically. Buds plump and very sticky. Leaves mid-green; palmate, with 5–7 toothed, stemless 'finger' leaflets, the broadest and longest one at the centre (up to 20cm long). Flowers 2cm across, white through to deep pink, borne on conical upright spikes, very obvious on tree. Fruit a large, round, glossy red-brown nut ('conker') inside a fleshy, spiny case.
DISTRIBUTION Native to the Balkans, but widely planted and naturalised across most of Europe.
LIFE CYCLE AND HABITAT Lives for more than 350 years. One of the 1st deciduous trees to come into leaf in spring, and develops autumn colours early as well. Parks, gardens and streets.

Holly ▪ *Ilex aquifolium* 8m (height)

DESCRIPTION Grows as a small, pointed-crowned tree or shrub; also commonly planted in hedges. Evergreen. Bark grey-brown, smooth but may be finely criss-crossed with small ridges and fissures. Leaves variable, up to 8cm long, usually with long, fine spikes along margin but sometimes smooth-edged; tough, very glossy on upperside, dark green (sometimes variegated, with creamy-white margins). Male flowers 4-petalled, 4-stamened, white. Female flowers (on separate tree) similar but with obvious green ovary and no stamens. Fruit (on female tree only) a scarlet berry borne in clusters.

DISTRIBUTION Widespread across NW Europe, becoming scarcer further E and barely reaching N Scandinavia.
LIFE CYCLE AND HABITAT Shade-tolerant, found as understorey in woodland and also in more exposed areas. Very widely planted as an ornamental tree or shrub, in parks, gardens and hedgerows.

Rowan ▪ *Sorbus aucuparia* 15m (height)

DESCRIPTION Dainty, round-crowned tree with a long, exposed trunk below 1st branches; also known as Mountain Ash. Foliage rather sparse. Bark smooth, dark. Leaves pinnate; 9–17 long, oval, stemless leaflets with serrated margins growing in opposite pairs, and single leaflet at stem tip. Green on upperside, grey-blue on underside. Flowers small, white, 4- or 5-petalled, with long stamens that give them a fluffy appearance; borne in very large, dense clusters (15cm across). Fruit an orange-red berry; borne in large, conspicuous clusters, very attractive to birds.
DISTRIBUTION Common and widespread across Europe.
LIFE CYCLE AND HABITAT Grows naturally in lowland and upland habitats, favouring woodlands but also able to survive on poor rocky soils in exposed situations. Very widely planted as a street tree, in parks and in gardens.

Swedish Whitebeam
▪ *Sorbus intermedia* 15m (height)

DESCRIPTION Small, oval-crowned deciduous tree. Trunk short, main branches angled upwards. Foliage dense, shaggy. Bark dark and rather smooth, similar to that of Rowan (above). Leaves superficially similar to oak leaves, up to 10cm long with large but shallowly indented round-edged lobes, long-stemmed, and leaf margin serrated; upperside deep green, shiny; underside grey and covered with down. Flowers small, 5-petalled, white, borne on broad flower head. Fruit orange or reddish, speckled.
DISTRIBUTION Native to S Sweden and the surrounding area; widely planted elsewhere in Europe.
LIFE CYCLE AND HABITAT A very tough, hardy tree. Thought to be a natural hybrid, with Common Whitebeam *S. aria*, Rowan and Wild Service Tree *S. torminalis* all involved in its ancestry. Can reproduce without pollination. Parks, gardens and roadsides, and woodlands where native.

Wild Cherry ■ *Prunus avium* 20m (height)

DESCRIPTION Oval deciduous tree with a short trunk. All branches angled quite steeply upwards. Foliage dense. Bark violet-brown, smooth with horizontal fissures that thicken with age. Leaves oval with pronounced point at tip, serrated along margins; up to 15cm long; glossy dark green with prominent network of veins, becoming very colourful in autumn. Flowers large, 3cm across, white, 5-petalled with prominent stamens – they appear before full foliage develops. Fruit a 2cm red or purplish cherry.

DESCRIPTION Found across most of Europe, including throughout the UK; in Sweden only reaches the S.

LIFE CYCLE AND HABITAT The ancestor of cultivated cherry trees, and widely planted in natural and cultivated forms. The tree is covered in blossom before leaves are fully grown. Thrives best in deep, rich soil. Parks, gardens, streets and woodland.

Common Hawthorn

■ *Crataegus monogyna* 10m (height)

DESCRIPTION Grows as a small, short-trunked and rounded tree or shrub, also in hedgerows. Deciduous. Foliage dense but irregular, compact around horizontally spreading branches. Bark grey-brown, with vertical fissures; outer stems very thorny. Leaves light green, darkening with age; up to 4cm long; broad-based with 5 or more very deeply cut lobes. Flowers white, 1cm across, 5-petalled with prominent dark stamens; grow profusely in loose clusters, giving whole plant a frosted appearance. Flowers mature into oval, 1cm-long red berry-like fruit ('haw'), much loved by many birds.

DISTRIBUTION Widespread and common across most of Europe, becoming scarcer further N.

LIFE CYCLE AND HABITAT Can live for hundreds of years. Flowers in mid-spring when the leaves are already out (giving rise to its alternative common names of May or May-blossom). Scrubland, woodland edges and hedgerows.

Common Lime
■ *Tilia × vulgaris* 45m (height)

DESCRIPTION Very tall deciduous tree, dome-shaped with a round crown and spreading base. Foliage dense, shaggy. Bark dull grey, becoming increasingly fissured with age and sprouting new leafy stems. Leaves large, broad and heart-shaped, often slightly asymmetrical, up to 15cm long, dark green with strong veins and toothed margin. Flowers small, green, borne in small clusters of 4 or more and attached to a narrow leaf-like bract. Fruit round, nut-like when mature, borne on a long stem from bract.

DISTRIBUTION Common across much of Europe, but rare or absent in N. Widely planted outside of its natural range.

LIFE CYCLE AND HABITAT Lives for up to 500 years. A naturally occurring hybrid between Large-leaved (*T. platyphyllos*) and Small-leaved (*T. cordata*) Lime trees. Flowers in midsummer; the flowers are very attractive to bees. Parks, gardens and streets.

Buddleia
■ *Buddleja davidii* 4m (height)

DESCRIPTION Dense, spreading deciduous shrub. Bark brown, rough and peeling in vertical strips. Leaves long and narrow, slightly twisting and with wavy edges, margins finely toothed. Dark green above, with deeply cut veins; underside white and downy. Flowers tiny, borne in dense, elongated clusters up to 30cm long at stem tips, spraying out and defining overall shape of shrub. Normal form lilac-purple, but white, deep violet and brighter pink forms also occur. Flowers highly fragrant, attracting butterflies and other insects. Flower head matures into a brown seed head.

DISTRIBUTION Native of E Asia, widely planted and naturalised in many European towns and cities, especially in the UK.

LIFE CYCLE AND HABITAT Tough and versatile, quickly colonising waste ground such as railway embankments and building sites. Flowers throughout midsummer. Gardens, parks, streets and wasteland.

Dogwood

■ *Cornus sanguinea* 5m (height)

DESCRIPTION Broad, dense, widely spreading deciduous shrub. Bark dark greenish brown or reddish brown; stem tips sometimes strikingly orange in winter. Leaves oval, up to 8cm long; smooth at margins but deep venation giving them a somewhat wrinkled appearance; bright yellow-green on upperside, paler on underside, becoming dark reddish in autumn. Flowers 4-petalled, small (1cm across) and creamy white; petals long and pointed; stamens prominent; borne in small, flat clusters; scent unpleasant. Flowers mature into blue-black round berries.

DISTRIBUTION Common across most of Europe, thinning out beyond N England and S Sweden.

LIFE CYCLE AND HABITAT Flowers in late spring to early summer. Found most commonly on chalky soils, and although it is somewhat tolerant of shade it thrives in full sunshine. Scrubland and downland; quite widely planted in parks and gardens.

Common Privet

■ *Ligustrum vulgare* 7m (height)

DESCRIPTION Broadly spreading, branching shrub, also found in hedgerows. Foliage thick, stems upright. Bark mid-greenish brown with fine vertical fissures. Leaves oval, narrow and elongated (up to 6cm long), tough and leathery, smooth surface and margins, mid-green with prominent midrib. Flowers small, white, 4-petalled with 2 yellow-tipped stamens at centre, borne in tapering clusters at stem tips. Fruits mature into green-centred black berries, 1cm across, borne in erect clusters and often remaining on plant well into winter.

DISTRIBUTION Widespread across most of Europe and naturalised further N as far as central Sweden.

LIFE CYCLE AND HABITAT This species and other close relatives are very popular garden hedging plants; it also grows wild in scrubland and at woodland edges. The foliage is eaten by many different moth species.

Elder ■ *Sambucus nigra* 7m (height)

DESCRIPTION Small, broad deciduous tree or shrub, often rather flat-topped. Dense twigs and branches, thick foliage. Bark light greyish, often very deeply fissured and ridged. Leaves pinnate, with normally 5 but up to 9 leaflets in opposite pairs and single leaflet at end of stem; leaflets short-stemmed, oval, pointed at tip and with toothed margins. Flower small, 5-petalled, white or creamy yellow; borne on large, umbrella-shaped, branching flower heads; smell strong and fairly pleasant. Fruit round, berry-like, borne in large, branched clusters that are more pendulous than the flower heads.

DISTRIBUTION Found across most of Europe, including the whole of the UK and into central Sweden.

LIFE CYCLE AND HABITAT Flowers appear in early summer and berries in Jul. Requires sunny conditions to flourish and flower. Often found at woodland margins and in scrubland.

Honeysuckle

■ *Lonicera periclymenum* 6m (length)

DESCRIPTION Woody creeping or climbing deciduous plant that twines around low trees and old tree stumps. Foliage often rather sparse. Bark grey. Leaves up to 6cm long, oval with pointed tip and short stalk, margins smooth, dark green with well-defined veins. Flowers up to 6cm long, with very long, narrow corolla tube that opens out into a broad petal on top and narrower petal below, often rolling back; cluster of stamens and long stigma project from tube; whitish with yellow or pink flush; borne in clusters at stem ends. Fruit a red berry, borne in clusters.

DISTRIBUTION Widespread and common in NW Europe, just reaching SW Sweden. Widely cultivated.

LIFE CYCLE AND HABITAT Tolerant of shade, and has a prolonged flowering season. Very fragrant at night, attracting moths. Woodlands and gardens.

Ivy ■ *Hedera helix* 20m (height)

DESCRIPTION Woody evergreen climbing plant that grows vigorously up walls and trees to reach light. Foliage variable but can be very dense. Bark greyish or reddish, rough-textured. Stems produce short, tufty anchoring roots as they climb. Leaves 3- or 5-lobed (diamond-shaped on flowering branches), tough, glossy, dark green; up to 10cm long. Variegated and golden-leaved cultivars also occur. Flowers small, yellow-green, borne in round clusters. Flowers develop into bluish-black berry-like fruit.
DISTRIBUTION Common across most of Europe, but in Sweden only in the S.
LIFE CYCLE AND HABITAT Grows up tall tree trunks, often cloaking the entire tree with its foliage and occasionally causing the tree to collapse under its weight. Also grows along the ground. Flowers late in the year, in early autumn, providing nectar for late-flying insects. Woods, parks and gardens.

Stinging Nettle
■ *Urtica dioica* 150cm (height)

DESCRIPTION Tall, upright herbaceous perennial plant, forming dense clumps. Stems reddish green, unbranched, covered with fine hairs. Leaves oval, broader at base and with pointed tip, up to 6cm long, margin deeply serrated, dark green and paler below, covered with short bristles and long stinging hairs. Separate male and female plants, both bearing tiny whitish flowers without visible petals on long, drooping catkins that sprout from leaf bases; female flower has feathery stigma; male flower has 4 long-stemmed stamens.
DISTRIBUTION Common and widespread throughout Europe.
LIFE CYCLE AND HABITAT Grows in many different situations, and is quite tolerant of shade. Important larval foodplant for many butterflies and other insect species. Stinging hairs on leaves help deter larger herbivores. Gardens, woodland edges, hedgerows, alongside rivers or by lakes, and waste ground.

Redshank
■ *Persicaria maculosa* 100cm (height)

DESCRIPTION Upright, branching annual plant. Stems green with a distinct red flush, branching, smooth. Leaves long (up to 10cm), narrow, oval with pointed tip and tapering at base, and almost stemless. Dark green, often marked with arrow-shaped dark smudge on centre, pointing towards tip of leaf. Flowers small, pink or whitish pink with large, pink-tipped stamens; borne on dense, upright flower spikes at stem tips.
DISTRIBUTION Widespread across most of Europe, becoming more scattered N of central Sweden.
LIFE CYCLE AND HABITAT Flowers in early summer through to late autumn. Grows in a wide variety of situations; was formerly a significant agricultural weed, but has become rarer since the advent of powerful herbicides. Usually found on bare ground and often near water, and may appear in gardens, parks and waste ground.

Black Bindweed
■ *Fallopia convolvulus* 2m (length)

DESCRIPTION Not to be confused with the true bindweeds, and also known as Wild Buckwheat. Creeping and climbing annual plant. Stems dull, light green, twining clockwise around other vegetation. Leaves heart- or arrowhead-shaped, up to 6cm long, dark green and glossy, pale yellow-green on underside. Flowers dull, dark green with narrow whitish wings, borne in small, loose clusters on long, leafed flower stems that sprout from leaf bases. Flowers form small, triangular fruit with wings, each containing 1 seed.
DISTRIBUTION Common and widespread across Europe.
LIFE CYCLE AND HABITAT Used centuries ago as a food crop but today more often regarded as a damaging agricultural and garden weed. Commonest on agricultural land but also occurs in waste ground, along embankments and roadsides, and in gardens.

Broad-leaved Dock

■ *Rumex obtusifolius* 50cm (height)

DESCRIPTION Tall, upright, unbranching perennial plant. Stems red-green, smooth. Leaves very large and long, especially at base of plant, where they may reach 45cm in length; oval, broader at base, with blunt tip and wavy margin. Basal leaves also have reddish stems. Separate male and female flowers on the same plant, both green becoming red, growing in clusters at intervals up a single stalk (which is sometimes branched) and projecting well clear of the leaves below. Fruit a small red-brown winged seed.

DISTRIBUTION Common and widespread across Europe, its distribution becoming more patchy N of central Sweden.

LIFE CYCLE AND HABITAT Flowers in early summer, although the flowers may be seen until early autumn. Wind-dispersed and quick to colonise bare and disturbed ground. May be found in almost all habitats.

Fat Hen ■ *Chenopodium album* 150cm (height)

DESCRIPTION Tall, upright, unbranching annual plant with a narrow profile. Stems mid-green, often with a whitish mealy dust covering. Shape of leaves varies: may be smooth-edged or with large, irregular, well-spaced serrations on margin, and usually long and narrow with pointed tip; also have a dusty white covering. Flowers tiny, with 5 green sepals, 5 short, yellow-tipped stamens and large, round green ovary; borne in bulbous, lumpy clusters, these sometimes branching clear and sometimes hugging stem from near base up to tip.

DISTRIBUTION Widespread throughout the whole of Europe.

LIFE CYCLE AND HABITAT Flowers from early summer through to autumn. Pioneering plant, quick to colonise newly disturbed ground; it is considered a significant agricultural weed in some areas, although in others it is itself cultivated for consumption. Farmland and waste ground.

Red Goosefoot
■ *Chenopodium rubrum* 80cm (height)

DESCRIPTION Tall, usually erect, annual herbaceous plant. Stems red-brown, smooth. Leaves diamond-shaped, much larger near base of stem; irregularly and deeply toothed; mid-green but often with reddish tinge, especially at margins; up to 9cm long. Flowers small and green with white-tipped stamens; borne in clusters on long stems that sprout from leaf bases from far down the main stem up to tip. Fruit is a seed at the centre of a papery circular wing.
DISTRIBUTION Occurs throughout much of Europe, becoming scarcer and more scattered in N UK, Ireland and N Sweden.
LIFE CYCLE AND HABITAT A late flowerer, blooming Aug–Oct. Soon colonises freshly disturbed ground by virtue of its windborne seeds. Waste ground, manure heaps, and edges of lakes and rivers; particularly prevalent near the sea.

Common Chickweed
■ *Stellaria media* 40cm (height)

DESCRIPTION Inconspicuous, spreading and often prostrate, small annual plant. Stems green, delicate, with hairs down 1 side only. Leaves oval and squat, with long stem and clearly pointed tip, in opposite pairs near base of stem and in rosettes around flowers. Flowers small, 5-petalled, white, each petal deeply divided into 2 lips; 5 green sepals (as long as or longer than petals) show between petals; 5 dark-tipped stamens and green around central ovary also visible; borne in small clusters at stem tips. Fruit a capsule containing numerous tiny seeds.
DISTRIBUTION Very common and widespread across the whole of Europe.
LIFE CYCLE AND HABITAT Flowers and produces seeds throughout the year. Occurs in nearly all open habitats, including gardens, waste ground, alongside paths and rivers, in parkland flowerbeds and even in flowerpots.

Red Campion

■ *Silene dioica* 90cm (height)

DESCRIPTION Tall, unbranched biennial or perennial. Stems green, becoming redder towards tip; hairy. Leaves oval with pointed tip, up to 8cm long, mid-green with pinkish tinge, covered in fine hairs; grow in opposite pairs up stem. Flowers 5-petalled; deep, rich, bright pink; petals broad with deep or shallow central split or indentation. Male and female flowers grow on separate plants; stamens and stigma short and inconspicuous on both, but flower base (covered with reddish hairy sepals) cylindrical in male flowers, very rotund in female flowers. Fruit an oval capsule full of small seeds.
DISTRIBUTION Common and widespread throughout most of Europe, including N Scandinavia.
LIFE CYCLE AND HABITAT A woodland and wayside flower, blooming in late spring to early summer. Thrives best in damp, nutrient-rich soil. Sunny spots in damp woodland areas.

White Campion

■ *Silene latifolia* 80cm (height)

DESCRIPTION Very closely related to Red Campion (above) and similar to it in many respects. Entire plant save for flowers covered in dense, rather sticky hair. Flowers white rather than red, with yellowish underside; usually larger than those of Red Campion, with longer stamens in male flowers. Flower base more inflated than in Red Campion and petals usually with deeper notches. Hybridises with Red Campion where both occur commonly; hybrids exhibit intermediate petal colours.
DISTRIBUTION Widespread and common across most of Europe, becoming more patchy in Ireland and in the far N of Sweden and Scotland.
LIFE CYCLE AND HABITAT Flowers from late spring into early autumn. Flowers open up fully at night. Found in most open habitats, especially those with rich soils. Woodland edges, along hedgerows, in set-aside fields and on waste ground.

Creeping Buttercup
■ *Ranunculus repens* 50cm (height)

DESCRIPTION Perennial herbaceous plant, producing both prostrate running stems and upright flowering stems. Leaves broad, up to 8cm long, largest at base of plant, smaller and narrower further up; divided into 3 large lobes, these further divided into smaller lobes. Both stems and leaves are covered with fine hair, leaves also sometimes spotted with white. Flowers 5-petalled; petals broad and blunt-ended, bright yellow and very shiny. Numerous yellow stamens at centre of flower. Fruit a cluster of simple seeds.
DISTRIBUTION Common and widespread across the whole of Europe.
LIFE CYCLE AND HABITAT Flowers May–Sep. Is distasteful to grazing animals, and prospers and spreads in fields where the surrounding grass is grazed or mown short. Farmland, waste ground and gardens.

Lesser Celandine
■ *Ranunculus ficaria* 20cm (height)

DESCRIPTION Perennial plant. Spreads itself mainly through 'breeder roots' that develop in the leaf bases; can carpet large areas. Stems fragile, light green, not hairy. Leaves slightly asymmetrical, rounded or heart-shaped, fleshy and shiny, borne on long stem, usually dark green but can look patchy. Flowers stand well clear of leafy mat; bright yellow (fading to white when older), with 8–12 slender, round-tipped, very shiny petals; cluster of yellow stamens at centre; 3 sepals.
DISTRIBUTION Common and widespread across most of Europe, reaching as far N as central Sweden.
LIFE CYCLE AND HABITAT An early-blooming flower of shady areas, first appearing in Mar and finished by May. Flowers close up when the sun goes in. Woodlands, meadows, riversides and other areas with rich, damp soil.

Hairy Bittercress
▪ *Cardamine hirsuta* 20cm (height)

DESCRIPTION Coarsely hairy annual plant. Flower stems erect, branching from rosette of leaves at base. Basal leaves pinnate, with 5 or more leaflets in opposite pairs and larger terminal leaflet at tip. Leaflets round or oval, fleshy, borne on short stems. A few leaves grow further up flower stems – these are also pinnate but leaflets are narrower and smaller. Flowers small, white, 4-petalled, borne in small clusters at end of flower stems. Flowers mature into long, slender fruits, these extending above tops of stems and containing numerous seeds.
DISTRIBUTION Common and widespread across most of Europe, but not found beyond S Sweden.
LIFE CYCLE AND HABITAT Flowers Feb–Nov. Ripe seed pods burst when touched, firing seeds considerable distances. Favours disturbed ground, including flowerbeds, farmland and waste ground.

Hedge Mustard
▪ *Sisymbrium officinale* 60cm (height)

DESCRIPTION Tall, rather hairy, branching, stiff-stemmed, upright annual or biennial. Flower stems grow from a basal central rosette of leaves. Basal leaves roughly pinnate, their leaflets becoming increasingly lobed and fusing towards end of leaf stem. Leaves at base of each flower stem much smaller, coarsely lobed, often T-shaped; margins coarsely toothed. Flowers small, 4-petalled, yellow. Flowers mature into long pods with tapered tips; flower stems comprise a few flowers at tip and upward-pointing pods hugging the stem all the way to the base.
DISTRIBUTION Common and widespread across most of Europe, thinning out into N Scotland and central Sweden.
LIFE CYCLE AND HABITAT Flowers continuously from May to Sep. Favours disturbed and bare ground, and is common along hedgerows, meadow edges, riverbanks, roadsides and waste ground.

Shepherd's Purse
▪ *Capsella bursa-pastoris* 35cm (height)

DESCRIPTION Annual or biennial. Flower stems upright and branching, growing from a rosette of basal leaves. These leaves are long, short-stemmed and usually deeply lobed or toothed, almost pinnate (especially towards base of leaf stem), asymmetrical and rough. Leaves on flower stem stalkless, long and narrow, often unlobed. Flowers small, white, 4-petalled, with yellow-tipped stamens, quite long corolla and 4 upright sepals. Flowers mature into heart-shaped flat fruits on long stems, so flower stems have flowers at tip and fruits maturing all the way down.
DISTRIBUTION Common and widespread across Europe.
LIFE CYCLE AND HABITAT May be seen in flower at any time of year. Grows in sunny situations on disturbed soil; common in arable fields, roadsides, flowerbeds, riverbanks and similar open places.

Garlic Mustard
▪ *Alliaria petiolata* 100cm (height)

DESCRIPTION Lush, leafy, clump-forming annual or biennial, with branching, upright flower stems. Leaves heart-shaped, larger and longer-stemmed towards base of plant, where they form a rosette; strongly toothed margin and prominent network of veins; bright, rich green above, hairy underneath. Flowers rather small, white, with 4 well-separated, rounded petals and 4 shorter green sepals; borne in clusters at stem tips. Flowers mature into long, slender, tapering pods containing oval black seeds.
DISTRIBUTION Common and widespread across most of Europe, reaching as far N as central Sweden.
LIFE CYCLE AND HABITAT Flowers Apr–Jul. Leaves produce a strong scent of garlic when crushed or trampled, although the plant is unrelated to garlic. Found in shady spots at a wide range of altitudes, in woodlands, hedgerows, parks and gardens.

Dog Rose
■ *Rosa canina* 3m (height/length)

DESCRIPTION Rambling woody deciduous plant. Younger stems green with a pink flush, covered in evenly spaced, backward-pointing hooked thorns, these pink when fresh and becoming duller with age. Leaves pinnate, with 5 or 7 leaflets of even size, dark green, strongly veined and with toothed margins. Flowers a large, simple, open, 5-petalled, pale pink (sometimes lighter or darker) rose; petals broad with single notch at tip; numerous yellow-orange stamens. Flowers mature into pear-shaped (but broader at base) red rosehips. DISTRIBUTION Widespread across most of NW Europe, just reaching into S Sweden. LIFE CYCLE AND HABITAT Grows along and up other vegetation, its hooked thorns helping it to climb. Flowers appear in Jun or Jul. Found in hedgerows, along woodland edges, and in parks and gardens.

Bramble
■ *Rubus fruticosus* 2m (height/length)

DESCRIPTION Scrambling, climbing woody deciduous plant. Stems very thorny, including flower and leaf stems. Leaves pinnate, with 3–7 large, oval leaflets, their margins strongly toothed; dark green above and covered with whitish down underneath. Flowers medium-sized, resembling a miniature rose; whitish to pale pink, occasionally with stronger pink flush; 5-petalled; numerous dark-tipped stamens clustered in centre. Flowers mature into cluster fruits – the familiar blackberry, though they are green at first and then red, before reaching their mature glossy black stage. DISTRIBUTION Found throughout most of Europe. LIFE CYCLE AND HABITAT Flowers May–Aug, with ripe fruit appearing from late summer into Oct. Grows vigorously and rapidly year-round. Forms dense thickets and spreads through creeping shoots. Found in woodlands, hedgerows, parks, wasteland and gardens.

Silverweed ■ *Potentilla anserina* Creeping

DESCRIPTION Creeping perennial. Stems reddish, hairy, prostrate, extending from main basal rosette of leaves. Leaves pinnate with numerous leaflets spaced alternately and single terminal leaf. Leaflets strongly toothed, silver-green with paler undersides, hairy on both surfaces. Flowers yellow, shiny, 5- or 6-petalled, with cluster of yellow stamens in centre; petals broad but narrow at base, leaving gaps there through which sepals are visible. Fruit contains round brown seeds.

DISTRIBUTION Widespread across Europe, but becoming scarcer in the far N.

LIFE CYCLE AND HABITAT Flowers May–Aug. Often associated with areas where waterfowl roost on lake banks (hence species name *anserina*, after the grey goose genus *Anser*), as it thrives in the nitrogen-rich conditions provided by the birds' droppings. Also found in meadows, verges and other grassy habitats.

Wood Avens
■ *Geum urbanum* 50cm (height)

DESCRIPTION Also known as Herb Bennet. Delicate, hairy, branching perennial. Stems green with fine hairs. Leaves lobed or sometimes fully divided to become pinnate, with 1–5 lobes/leaflets (basal leaves more often pinnate than lobed); oval with pointed tips and strongly toothed margins; mid-green, paler below. Flowers yellow, 5-petalled, with long, pointed sepal tips showing between petals; mass of yellow stamens at flower centre. Flower stems erect but becoming drooping. Flowers mature into cluster of fruits, each with a hooked hair at tip.

DISTRIBUTION Common and widespread across Europe, but not reaching beyond central Sweden.

LIFE CYCLE AND HABITAT Flowers Jun–Aug. Fruits hook onto fur of passing animals and can thus be widely distributed. Found in sheltered, sometimes shady spots in woodlands, parks and gardens.

Tufted Vetch
■ *Vicia cracca* 120cm (height)

DESCRIPTION Perennial plant of the pea family.
Stems green with reddish tinge; some prostrate.
Leaves pinnate, with opposite pairs of small,
narrow, pointed green leaflets. There is no terminal
leaflet, but 2 or more long, fine, twisting tendrils
instead. Flower colour varies from blue through
various shades of pink and violet. Flower shape
typical of family: longish corolla with broad upper
petal shading smaller, lip-like petals below. Up to
40 flowers arranged in single line up flower stem.
Flowers mature into short, hairless brown pods,
each containing a few round seeds.
DISTRIBUTION Common and widespread
throughout Europe.
LIFE CYCLE AND HABITAT Flowers Jun–Aug.
Leaf tendrils wind around surrounding vegetation,
helping the plant to scramble and spread. Verges,
meadows, woodland edges and waste ground.

White Clover
■ *Trifolium repens* 45cm (height)

DESCRIPTION Creeping perennial of the pea
family. Stems delicate; flower stems upright,
otherwise prostrate and tougher. Leaves pinnate,
with 3 leaflets arranged evenly at stem tip. Leaflets
mid- or dark green with small white 'V' marking at
centre, pointing towards leaflet tip. Flowers white,
pinkish towards base, small, shape typical of family.
Arranged in round clusters on flower heads, often
with a distinct division between downward-angled
lower flowers and upward-angled upper flowers.
Flowers mature into small, unobtrusive pods.
DISTRIBUTION Common and widespread
throughout Europe.
LIFE CYCLE AND HABITAT Flowers May–Sep.
Often forms dense carpets on open grassy areas, the
prostrate stems developing new roots as they spread.
Individuals with 4 leaflets rather than 3 occasionally
occur, and are regarded as lucky. Grassy areas, from
lawns and verges to set-aside fields.

Herb Robert
■ *Geranium robertianum* 40cm (height)

DESCRIPTION Straggling and branching annual or biennial plant with shallow roots. Stems delicate, reddish and hairy. Leaves long-stemmed, deeply lobed into 3–7 sections that are themselves very deeply toothed or lobed; green but becoming red with age, hairy. Flowers with 5 round, light or deep pink petals; 10 small stamens clustered in centre. Fruit hairy, pear-shaped pod with very long, protruding 'beak'.
DISTRIBUTION Common and widespread across most of Europe, reaching NE Sweden.
LIFE CYCLE AND HABITAT Flowers May–Oct. When the seed pods are ripe, their sides spring back, firing the seeds high in the air. This, plus the shallow rooting system, means plants may be found growing in the branch forks of moss-covered trees. Found in a wide range of habitats, including in towns.

Dove's-foot Crane's-bill
■ *Geranium molle* 25cm (height)

DESCRIPTION Short, very hairy, branching annual. Stems covered in long hairs; flowering stems erect, others prostrate. Leaves almost round, with palmate radiating veins; lobed into up to 7 broad segments, with all segments further lobed. Leaves form a rosette at base of plant and are single or in opposite pairs on flowering shoots; basal leaves long-stemmed. Flowers have 5 broad, pale pink or pale violet notched petals, with clear dark veins extending from base; stamens and stigma clustered in centre. Long sepals may show between petals. Fruit a pod with a long, protruding 'beak'.
DISTRIBUTION Found across most of Europe, including S Sweden.
LIFE CYCLE AND HABITAT Flowers Apr–Sep. Grows in bare or grassy ground in sunny situations, including riverbanks, waste ground and dry, rocky fields.

Petty Spurge
■ *Euphorbia peplus* 30cm (height)

DESCRIPTION Small, branching, rather bushy
annual. One of the smaller of several rather similar
spurge species. Stems yellowish green, hairless.
Leaves oval with rounded tip, short-stemmed and
small, margins smooth; grow alternately up stem,
with an opposite stemless leaf pair immediately
below flowering heads. Flowers bright yellow-green,
indistinct (look like freshly forming young leaves),
long-stemmed, with 4 rounded petals. Male and
female flowers are separate. Seed capsule small
and green.

DISTRIBUTION Widespread across most of
Europe, reaching as far N as central Sweden.
LIFE CYCLE AND HABITAT May be seen in flower
at any time of year. Grows on cultivated arable
land and gardens, and can be an invasive and
problematic weed. Also found on other disturbed
ground and marginal habitats, such as street cracks.

Sweet Violet ■ *Viola odorata* 10cm (height)

DESCRIPTION Small, delicate perennial. Stems
mid-green, slender. Leaves grow in a basal rosette,
lush mid-green, slightly crinkled-looking and glossy,
heart-shaped, rounded at tip, about as wide as
they are long, margins with subtle rounded teeth.
Flowers 5-petalled with 2 broad upper petals and
3 lower petals, central one extending back into
a pouch-like spur; all dark violet-purple with
darker veins and white bases (occasionally, petals
are all white), nodding on slender flower stem;
sweetly fragrant; corolla longish, stamens visible
at base of central lower petal. Fruit a capsule in
3 segments.

DISTRIBUTION Fairly common across most
of Europe, but not found N of central Scotland
or central Sweden.
LIFE CYCLE AND HABITAT Flowers in early
to mid-spring; requires nutrient-rich soils. Grows
in sheltered places – woodland verges and paths,
parks, cemeteries and gardens.

Common Dog Violet
■ *Viola riviniana* 15cm

DESCRIPTION Small, attractive perennial plant. Closely resembles the Sweet Violet (p. 129), but leaves grow further up stems rather than being concentrated in a basal rosette. Leaves heart-shaped with very rounded teeth along margins. Flowers lack the sweet fragrance of Sweet Violet, and are often slightly lighter and cooler in colour (becoming especially pale on the spur), with more prominent dark veins, especially on the lower central petal; borne on long, delicate, hairless stems. Also, Sweet Violet has blunt-tipped sepals while those of Dog Violet have pointed tips. DISTRIBUTION Fairly common across most of Europe, reaching into N Sweden.

LIFE CYCLE AND HABITAT Flowers Mar–May. Its common name reflects its perceived inferiority to Sweet Violet. Found in similar habitats to Sweet Violet, along woodland rides and in clearings, by hedgerows and in other sheltered places.

Rosebay Willowherb
■ *Epilobium angustifolium* 150cm (height)

DESCRIPTION Very striking, tall, erect, unbranched perennial. Stems smooth, sturdy; green with red flush, this becoming stronger towards tip. Leaves long, narrow and pointed, rich green above and silver-green below, angled upwards but often drooping at tips, alternating up stem as far as lowest flowers. Flowers with very long corolla; 4-petalled, with top 2 petals larger; bright, rich pink, fading towards petal edges; stamens whitish with dark red tips, drooping; stigma longer than stamens, splits at tip into 4 short branches. Flowers grow up to stem tip, with the most mature flowers furthest down. Fruit a very long, slim pod, containing fluffy seeds. DISTRIBUTION Very common and widespread throughout Europe.
LIFE CYCLE AND HABITAT Flowers in midsummer. Seeds are wind-dispersed; soon colonises new habitats. Woodland clearings, riversides and waste ground.

Hoary Willowherb

■ *Epilobium parviflorum* 80cm (height)

DESCRIPTION Fairly tall, unbranching, erect perennial. Stems green, covered in stiff hairs. Leaves long, narrow, stemless, with slightly toothed margins; grow in a basal rosette and then in opposite pairs up stem but not hugging it, up to and beyond 1st flowers. Flowers small, light purple or pink, with 4 broad petals that are strongly notched; broadly 4-branched stigma tip prominent in flower centre. Flowers mature into long, slender, pod-like fruit capsules.
DISTRIBUTION Found across most of Europe, almost reaching the N edge of Scotland but not beyond S Sweden.
LIFE CYCLE AND HABITAT Flowers Jul–Aug. Pollinated by bees and hoverflies. Requires damp but well-drained soil in sunny situations, so is often associated with wetland habitats such as lake shores, streamsides and riverbanks.

Ground Elder

■ *Aegopodium podagraria* 60cm (height)

DESCRIPTION Fairly tall, branching perennial plant. Despite its common name is not related to Elder trees (p. 116) but is a member of the carrot family. Stems fresh green, ridged and hairless. Leaves deep green, broad, oval, large and long-stalked, becoming narrower, smaller and shorter-stalked further up stems; margins slightly toothed. Flowers very small, 5-petalled, each petal rounded and notched, stamens long; borne on dense, branched, umbrella-shaped heads, on long stems that stand well clear of the highest leaves. Fruit a small green capsule.
DISTRIBUTION Widespread across Europe as far NE as central Sweden, beyond which it is more scattered.
LIFE CYCLE AND HABITAT Flowers Jun–Jul. Grows at most altitudes in damp, sheltered and somewhat shady places, such as woodland edges, along riverbanks and at the base of hedgerows.

Primrose
▪ *Primula vulgaris* 20cm (height)

DESCRIPTION Clump-forming perennial. Stems slender, red-green and covered in fine hairs. Leaves long, rich green, oval, broader towards tip and tapering towards stem, with prominent broad midrib and crinkled appearance; margins wavy; forms rosettes. Flowers large, with 5 broad petals, these flat or slightly notched at outer edge; light yellow, deepening at base; borne singly on long, hairy, leafless stems. At centre of petals is a neat, round hole in which either stigma or stamens are clearly visible (though all flowers possess both structures). Fruit a capsule containing black seeds.
DISTRIBUTION Fairly common in NW Europe, becoming patchy further E; not in Sweden.
LIFE CYCLE AND HABITAT Flowers Mar–Jun. Grows in sheltered, shady spots, including woodland paths and edges, and hedgerows.

Cowslip ▪ *Primula veris* 25cm (height)

DESCRIPTION Perennial, similar to Primrose (above) in some ways and hybridises with it to produce intermediate-looking **False Oxlip**, or **Polyanthus** *P. veris* × *vulgaris*, which is now a popular garden plant in various colour forms. Leaves similar to that of Primrose, but less crinkled-looking. Flowers 5-petalled, bright yellow with orange streak in centre at base; corolla long and plump, giving flower a bell shape, the base enclosed by long sepals; borne in small, nodding clusters at end of long, unbranching stem. Fruit a cylindrical capsule.
DISTRIBUTION Fairly common in NW Europe, but not reaching beyond central Sweden or to the far N of Scotland.
LIFE CYCLE AND HABITAT Flowers Apr–Jun. Generally prefers more open habitats than Primrose, and requires chalky or lime-rich soil. Meadows, downland, sunny woodland rides or clearings and scrubland.

Creeping Jenny
■ *Lysimachia nummularia* Creeping

DESCRIPTION Prostrate, spreading perennial. Stems slender; ground-running stems paler and sturdier. Leaves bright, deep green, small, broad, oval (almost round), smooth with subtle venation, borne on short stems (plant's common alternative name of Moneywort is derived from coin-like appearance of leaves). Flowers dainty, 5-petalled; petals bright, shiny yellow with pointed tips; orange-tipped yellow stamens protrude from flower centre; grow singly from bases of leaf stems. Fruit a 5-segmented capsule. DISTRIBUTION Widespread across most of Europe; rare to absent in most of Scotland; patchy in Ireland, and in Sweden only reaching S.
LIFE CYCLE AND HABITAT Flowers May–Jul. Seed is blown from pods by the wind, giving the plant good dispersal powers. Grows on nutrient-rich, damp soils in a very wide range of habitats, including riversides, ditches, woodlands and road verges.

Scarlet Pimpernel
■ *Anagallis arvensis* Creeping

DESCRIPTION Creeping, clump-forming annual. Stems long and weak, smooth, prostrate or sprawling. Leaves fresh green above, paler below with a scattering of darker spots; oval, fairly broad, with pointed tip and smooth margins; grow in opposite pairs along stem. Flowers 5-petalled; petals broad with blunt tips; deep, rich orange-red, flushing violet-pink at base; round opening to corolla, from which prominent yellow-tipped stamens emerge. Blue-petalled forms are occasionally seen. Flowers borne singly on long stems. Fruit a simple capsule. DISTRIBUTION Common across most of Europe, but more scattered in Scotland and N Sweden. LIFE CYCLE AND HABITAT Flowers Jun–Oct. Petals open only in sunshine and close by mid-afternoon. Grows on nutrient-rich soils in all kinds of habitats, from arable fields and roadside verges to gardens and parks.

Hedge Bindweed
■ *Calystegia sepium* 3m (length)

DESCRIPTION Climbing perennial. Stems sturdy and can be very long; smooth and green, becoming redder close to shoot tips. Leaves heart- or arrowhead-shaped, often with suggestion of pointed lobes close to base; grow in opposite pairs. Flowers large, white (sometimes with pinkish flush), comprised of 5 fused petals flaring out from longish corolla into trumpet shape; stamens and stigma visible at opening of corolla in centre. Fruit a squat brown papery capsule of seeds.
DISTRIBUTION Widespread and common across most of Europe, but scattered in N Sweden and the far N of Scotland.
LIFE CYCLE AND HABITAT Flowers Jun–Sep. New shoots twine anticlockwise around surrounding vegetation, fences and other obstacles. Prefers damp and nutrient-rich soil. Waste ground, hedgerows, woodland edges and any overgrown areas.

Common Cleavers
■ *Galium aparine* 2m (length)

DESCRIPTION Scrambling, climbing, branching annual, also known as Goosegrass. Entire plant is covered in very sticky hairs. Stems square in cross section, fresh green, very sturdy near base of plant. Leaves long and narrow (broadening slightly towards tip); margins smooth, with very fine, short point at otherwise rounded tip; stalkless; grow in whorls of 6–8 around stems at branching points. Flowers very small, white, 4-petalled with yellow-tipped stamens. Fruit a pair of large seeds with hairy skin.
DISTRIBUTION Widespread and common across most of Europe, reaching as far N as central Sweden.
LIFE CYCLE AND HABITAT Flowers Jun–Oct. Sticky hairs give it purchase to grow up and over surrounding vegetation. Seeds stick to clothing and animal fur. Requires good soil. Woodlands, hedgerows and gardens.

Common Comfrey
■ *Symphytum officinale* 100cm (height)

DESCRIPTION Tall, upright perennial. Stems
thick and sturdy, mid-green, covered in fine
hairs. Leaves broad and long, pointed at tip,
stalkless and hugging main stem at base; deep
and pronounced veins give them a wrinkled
look. Flowers long, bell-shaped; base of corolla
in pointed, hairy sepals; 5 petals with pointed
tips flaring slightly at ends; colour varies from
deep, rich purple through paler pinks or purples
to yellow-white; borne in nodding clusters.
Fruit a small capsule among the sepals.
DISTRIBUTION Common and widespread
across most of Europe, reaching as far N as
central Sweden.
LIFE CYCLE AND HABITAT Flowers May–Jul.
Attracts many insects, including bumblebees,
which cut through the corolla to reach the
nectar without pollinating the plant. Damp
areas, including riverbanks and woodlands.

Early Forget-me-not
■ *Myosotis ramosissima* 5cm (height)

DESCRIPTION Very small perennial plant. Stems
becoming fragile and droopy closer to tip, reddish
green, covered densely in fine hairs. Leaves oval,
broader towards base, blunt-tipped with smooth
margins, stalkless and closely hugging main stem;
grow in a basal rosette and then alternately up
stem until flower heads branch off. Flowers small,
5-petalled; light, bright blue, whitening towards
base, with yellow 'eye' ring around opening to
corolla. Sepals dark grey-green, fuzzy. Flowers
borne in small clusters at stem tips. Fruit a
small capsule surrounded by persisting sepals.
DISTRIBUTION Widespread and common across
most of Europe, but scattered in Ireland and the
far N of Scotland, and not reaching N Sweden.
LIFE CYCLE AND HABITAT Flowers in early
spring, from Mar. Grows on poor sandy soil,
bare or with grass, especially near coast.

Self-heal ▪ *Prunella vulgaris* 30cm (height)

DESCRIPTION Hairy, upright, non-branching perennial. Stems sturdy, fresh green, square in cross section and covered in fine hairs. Leaves oval, broader at base, especially hairy on underside. Main stem leaves angled upwards, long-stemmed. Leaves at base of flower head grow out horizontally and are stemless. Flowers similar to those of members of the pea family, with a hood formed of 2 fused upper petals, and a lip comprised of 3 fused lower petals; long corolla, from which white stamens project; colour varies from deep purple to almost white; borne in clusters at stem tips. 4 sticky fruitlets develop in remains of sepals.
DISTRIBUTION Common and widespread across Europe, becoming scattered in the far N of Sweden.
LIFE CYCLE AND HABITAT Flowers in midsummer. Found in diverse habitats, from damp woodland to lake shores and lawns.

Ground Ivy
▪ *Glechoma hederacea* 40cm (height)

DESCRIPTION Upright perennial with prostrate running stems, these covered in fine hairs. Stems fresh green, square in cross section. Leaves heart-shaped, broad; margin with large, round-edged teeth; grow in opposite pairs up stem, borne on short stalks. Flowers rather like those of members of the pea family, with narrow upper petals not strongly hooded, and 2 small 'wings' on either side of broad lower lip; mid-purple to light lilac, lip speckled with darker purple; borne in small clusters sprouting from leaf bases all the way up stem. Fruit develops within retained flower sepals.
DISTRIBUTION Widespread and common across Europe, becoming scattered in the far N of Sweden.
LIFE CYCLE AND HABITAT Flowers Apr–Jun. Found in many habitats on rich soils in reasonably sunny situations, including woodland paths and clearings, hedgerows, riversides, meadows and embankments.

White Dead-nettle
■ *Lamium album* 50cm (height)

DESCRIPTION Upright, hairy, non-branching perennial. Stems thick, green with reddish flush, covered in fine hairs. Leaves bear a close resemblance to those of Stinging Nettle (p. 117); oval, tapering to a pointed tip; short-stemmed (especially near top of plant), with strongly toothed margins; borne in opposite pairs up stem. Flowers white; similar in shape to those of members of the pea family, with top 2 petals forming an extended, overarching hood, below which is a downward-angled lip; borne in whorls up stem at leaf bases, but not at stem tip. Fruit comprises 4 parts.
DISTRIBUTION Common and widespread across Europe, but scattered in N Scotland, SW Ireland and N Sweden.
LIFE CYCLE AND HABITAT Flowers Apr–Oct. Often grows with Stinging Nettle (p. 117), though is itself stingless. Rich soils in woodlands, hedgerows, and alongside walls, ditches and fences.

Red Dead-nettle
■ *Lamium purpureum* 45cm (height)

DESCRIPTION Hairy, upright, non-branching annual. Stems square in cross section, hairy, reddish or greenish. Leaves oval or heart-shaped, broadest at base, covered in soft hairs and with strongly toothed margins; green, becoming reddish towards stem tip; borne in opposite pairs up stem, stalks long towards base of plant and much shorter towards stem tip. Flowers resemble those of members of the pea family, narrow when viewed head-on, with overarching hood and smaller, dark-spotted lip; borne in whorls up stem at leaf bases. Fruit in 4 parts.
DISTRIBUTION Common and widespread across most of Europe, becoming patchier in N Sweden.
LIFE CYCLE AND HABITAT Flowers Mar–Oct. Provides a valuable nectar source for early-flying insects. Most often found in freshly disturbed, rich soil, in vegetable gardens and other cultivated land.

Spearmint
■ *Mentha spicata* 100cm (height)

DESCRIPTION Tall, upright perennial, hairless or quite hairy. Entire plant smells strongly of mint. Stems green, quite sturdy. Leaves oval, quite large (up to 9cm), tapering at tip; rich, deep green, paler below; margins strongly toothed and tip pointed; short-stalked or almost stalkless; borne in opposite pairs. Flowers similar to those of members of the pea family, small with long projecting stamens and stigma, white or very pale pink; borne in a slender, slightly conical flower spike, with smaller spikes branching off main stem.
DISTRIBUTION Found across most of Europe; rarer in Scotland and Ireland, and in Sweden reaching only the S.
LIFE CYCLE AND HABITAT Flowers Jul–Oct. Commonly cultivated in herb gardens as well as being widely naturalised – the most popular garden mint. Prefers damp, sheltered places such as riverbanks and woodland clearings.

Bittersweet
■ *Solanum dulcamara* 100cm (height/length)

DESCRIPTION Scrambling, branching, downy perennial plant, also known as Woody Nightshade. Stems woody at base; some creeping, others climbing or erect. Leaves heart- or arrow-shaped, long (up to 20cm) with parallel edges and pointed tip, borne on longish stalk. Flowers have 5 narrow, pointed petals, deep violet with dark scales at base around opening of corolla, from which protrudes yellow cone of joined stamens around central stigma; borne in branching, nodding, small clusters. Fruit a smooth, glossy, oval berry, initially green, then yellow and finally red.
DISTRIBUTION Widespread across most of Europe, but scattered in N Scotland and N Sweden.
LIFE CYCLE AND HABITAT Flowers May–Sep. Climbs over surrounding vegetation. Found by ditches and rivers, in wet woodland and close to the sea.

Common Figwort

■ *Scrophularia nodosa* 70cm (height)

DESCRIPTION Upright, unbranched perennial. Stems sturdy, green with a tinge of red. Leaves oval, fairly broad, with a pointed tip and pronounced irregular toothing along margins; much larger towards base of stem; stalkless, growing in opposite pairs up stem. Flowers small, inconspicuous, borne on long stems; rotund corolla within sepals, small hood of reddish petals at top, small white lip below, and open 'throat' within which yellow stamens can be seen; borne in small, branching clusters at and near top of stem. Fruit a pear- or fig-shaped pod.
DISTRIBUTION Widespread across most of Europe, but not reaching N Sweden.
LIFE CYCLE AND HABITAT Flowers Jun–Sep, although only a few flowers open on a plant at any one time. Found in shady habitats with other lush vegetation.

Germander Speedwell

■ *Veronica chamaedrys* 40cm (height)

DESCRIPTION Erect, hairy perennial, the showiest of several speedwell species. Stems rather dark red-green, with hairs in 2 opposite rows. Leaves oval, broad, with deep-cut, round-edged teeth; grow in opposite pairs, short-stalked at base of plant and stalkless towards tip. Very short-lived flower 4-petalled; petals broad and round, deep violet-blue with fine darker veins (fading to pink with age), white at base, forming white ring around opening of short corolla; 2 long, fine white stamens protrude from corolla. Flowers borne in small clusters at or close to stem tip. Fruit a flattened, heart-shaped capsule.
DISTRIBUTION Widespread and common across most of Europe.
LIFE CYCLE AND HABITAT Flowers May–Jul. Spreads via creeping roots to form patches. Damp meadows and lawns, and glades, clearings and paths in woodland.

Foxglove
▪ *Digitalis purpurea* 150cm (height)

DESCRIPTION Tall, very striking, upright biennial. Stems thick, downy, unbranched. Leaves oval, deep green with downy grey underside, margins with rounded teeth, long stalk. Flowers long, broad, bell-shaped, opening out at tip to reveal wide 'throat'; usually deep, rich pink, becoming paler towards petal edges, with white-circled black spots in 'throat'; paler and white forms are not unusual. Flowers borne in long spikes of up to 100, on 1 side of stem; spikes project well above leaves. Fruit a squat capsule containing tiny seeds.
DISTRIBUTION Common across most of NW Europe, and naturalised in S Sweden.
LIFE CYCLE AND HABITAT Flowers Jun–Aug. Plants develop a basal leaf rosette in their 1st year and flower in the 2nd. Woodland clearings and rides, and sheltered spots in parks and gardens.

Greater Plantain
▪ *Plantago major* 30cm (height)

DESCRIPTION Upright perennial plant, one of several similar plantain species. Stems long and bare between basal leaves and flower head; downy; green, darkening towards tip. Leaves oval, with prominent longitudinal veins, pointed tip and long stalk; grow in a basal rosette only. Flowers very small, white, with quite long corolla, 4 short petal tips and 4 very long stamens that have large purplish or brownish heads; borne in densely packed flower spike at top of stem, this with a fluffy appearance owing to long stamens. Fruit a small grey seed capsule.
DISTRIBUTION Common and widespread across Europe.
LIFE CYCLE AND HABITAT Flowers Jun–Sep. Seeds sticky, carried on human and animal feet to new grounds. Prospers in open sites such as lawns and fields, and alongside paths and roads.

Wild Teasel

■ *Dipsacus fullonum* 2m (height)

DESCRIPTION Tall, branching, upright biennial. All parts of the plant are covered in spines. Stems ridged, thick, light green, with short, thorn-like spines. Leaves long and narrow, stemless, borne in opposite pairs; margins with short spines. Flowers tiny, showing 4 short petal tips and long stamens with large heads. Flower heads large, oval, with honeycomb-like structure; flowers emerging from holes, long spines at junctions of holes; ring of central flowers opens first. Very long, spear-like bracts at base of flower head. Fruit tiny seeds.
DISTRIBUTION Common and widespread across most of Europe.
LIFE CYCLE AND HABITAT Flowers Jul–Aug. Seed attracts Goldfinches (p. 38). Old seed heads persist through the winter. Grows along banks and paths, on waste ground and in other open places on good soil.

Daisy ■ *Bellis perennis* 15cm (height)

DESCRIPTION Small, downy, ground-hugging perennial. Stems mid-green, covered in fine down. Leaves oval, with smooth margins; grow in rosettes only at ground level. Flower heads are composite, borne on long, bare stem; composed of tiny yellow florets forming a round, spongy centre, surrounded by a ring of many long, narrow white (often pink-tipped) petals. Central florets mature into small fruitlets after outer ring of petals has fallen away.
DISTRIBUTION Common and widespread across most of Europe, but scattered in Sweden and N Scotland.
LIFE CYCLE AND HABITAT May be seen in flower at any time of the year. Flower heads close up overnight and during cool weather. One of the commonest, most familiar and most persistent lawn weeds; also grows in other close-cropped grassy environments.

Yarrow
■ *Achillea millefolium* 50cm (height)

DESCRIPTION Sturdy, strongly aromatic perennial. Stems thick and tough, green or reddish, downy. Plant also produces prostrate runners, by which it spreads. Leaves very much divided into multiple tips, almost feathery, mid-green, stalkless, growing alternately up stem from base (where they are largest). Composite flower small, with 4–6 rounded outer petals, white with a pink flush, and a cluster of tiny yellowish florets at centre; borne in dense clusters in spreading, umbrella-shaped heads, central composite flowers opening first. Flowers mature into dry brown fruits.
DISTRIBUTION Common and widespread across most of Europe.
LIFE CYCLE AND HABITAT Flowers Jun–Oct. Found at almost all altitudes and in a variety of habitats, including meadows, grazed pastures, waste ground and riverbanks.

Tansy ■ *Tanacetum vulgare* 120cm (height)

DESCRIPTION Distinctive, branching perennial. Stems strong, downy; green, but main stem dark reddish. Leaves pinnate, with up to 30 alternately spaced, very long, narrow leaflets with strongly toothed margins (tooth points blunt), becoming much shorter towards tip; overall leaf shape is fern-like. Composite flower head composed of a tightly packed cluster of small, bright yellow florets forming a round ball, with no outer ray-like petals; borne in quite dense, umbrella-shaped clusters at stem tips. Mature fruits blackish.
DISTRIBUTION Common and widespread across most of Europe, thinning out and becoming scattered in N Sweden.
LIFE CYCLE AND HABITAT Flowers Jul–Sep. Common on rocky waste ground and quick to colonise fire-damaged ground; also found on riverbanks, pathways and similar habitats.

Feverfew
▪ *Tanacetum parthenium* 60cm (height)

DESCRIPTION Sturdy, branching perennial. Stems green, downy. Leaves lobed or pinnate, divided into 3–6 sections on each side, these sections deeply toothed (tooth edges blunt). Composite flowers numerous at stem tips and superficially similar to those of Daisy (p. 141), with a round central cluster of small yellow florets surrounded by radiating white petals, these broader and fewer than in Daisy. Some cultivated varieties lack the outer white petals and thus resemble the flowers of Tansy (p. 142).
DISTRIBUTION Native to SE Europe, but widely naturalised in countries further N.
LIFE CYCLE AND HABITAT Flowers Jun–Aug. Widely cultivated ornamentally; its derivatives are used in migraine medication. Found in warm, sunny locations, on waste ground, field edges and among rocky scrubland.

Oxeye Daisy
▪ *Leucanthemum vulgare* 70cm (height)

DESCRIPTION Tall, striking, mostly unbranched perennial, also known as Marguerite. Stems dark green. Leaves slightly hairy, with long teeth on margins; lower leaves long-stalked; upper leaves alternate, shorter-stalked and sometimes stalkless. Composite flower looks like scaled-up version of Daisy flower (p. 141) but lacks pink edges to outer white petals; borne singly on long stems. Flower base contained in casing of overlapping green scales. Flowers mature into clusters of brown seeds, retained on stiff stems.
DISTRIBUTION Common and widespread throughout Europe.
LIFE CYCLE AND HABITAT Flowers Jun–Oct, forming especially striking shows in early summer. Attractive to nectar-feeding insects. Found in open, sunny situations on heavy soils – pastures, mountain fields and arable field margins, and sometimes even on lawns.

Winter Heliotrope
■ *Petasites fragrans* 30cm

DESCRIPTION Low-growing perennial. Stems covered in white down. Basal leaves green on top, downy and paler below; heart-shaped or rounded, and round at tip; margins with rounded, blunt teeth edged with black; appear after flowers. Leaves growing up flower stem are very different: small and scale-like, often tinged reddish, arranged alternately up stem. Flowers a Daisy-like composite with a round mass of central yellow florets; ray petals also yellow, shiny, narrow and very numerous (up to 300). Fruits bear tufts of soft, fluffy hairs to enable wind dispersal, seed head thus like Common Dandelion 'clock' (p. 146).
DISTRIBUTION Common and widespread across most of Europe, but scarcer in the far N of Sweden.
LIFE CYCLE AND HABITAT Flowers Mar–Apr. Exploits dry and stony ground, such as quarries and gravel workings, pathways and exposed chalky soil.

Common Ragwort
■ *Senecio jacobaea* 100cm (height)

DESCRIPTION Tall, sturdy, branching biennial or perennial. Stems strong, green, angular or ridged. Leaves grow alternately up stem, long and broad, largest towards base of plant; pinnate or lobed, with leaflets fusing towards tip, lobes/leaflets narrow at base and broadening; margins with rounded teeth. Flowers composite, with yellow florets forming a round central cluster and c. 12–15 narrow yellow outer petals surrounding it; borne in clusters at stem ends. Seed head bears seeds with fluffy tufts.
DISTRIBUTION Common and widespread across most of Europe; in Sweden, found in S and extending up coast.
LIFE CYCLE AND HABITAT Flowers Jul–Sep. Avoided by grazing mammals, so tall plants often seen in pastures. Also waste ground, embankments and similar habitats.

Groundsel  *Senecio vulgaris* 30cm (height)

DESCRIPTION Small, leafy, branching annual, similar to Common Ragwort (p. 144) in some respects. Stems relatively thick, green with white downy covering. Leaves long, narrow, roughly and unevenly lobed and toothed, often with covering of fine hairs; stalkless. Composite flower longer than it is wide, with long, narrow sepals containing most of its length; central florets bright yellow, projecting just beyond sepals; lacks outer radiating petals; borne in small clusters at stem tips. Mature seeds clustered together, with outer tufts of fluffy white hair.

DISTRIBUTION Common and widespread across most of Europe.

LIFE CYCLE AND HABITAT Flowers through most of the year, apart from midwinter. The windborne seeds sometimes germinate in gutters and roof cracks; also found in exposed situations in fields, gardens and waste ground.

Creeping Thistle
▪ *Cirsium arvense* 120cm (height)

DESCRIPTION Tall, branching, prickly perennial. One of several species of thistle – most other common species have larger or more deeply coloured flowers. Stems spineless; green, becoming darker and redder towards tips. Leaves oval, but thorny margin gives them an angular appearance; long spine at tip, stalkless; grow alternately up stem. Flowers composite, comprising numerous light purple florets, and long, fine ray petals creating a fluffy appearance; borne singly on stem tips. Mature fruiting heads are clusters of fluff-topped seeds.

DISTRIBUTION Common and widespread across most of Europe.

LIFE CYCLE AND HABITAT Flowers Jul–Sep. Flowers very attractive to butterflies and bees. Wind-dispersed seeds enable it to become quickly established in new habitats. Found in weedy patches, arable fields and pastures, riverbanks and waste ground.

Perennial Sow-thistle

■ *Sonchus arvensis* 150cm (height)

DESCRIPTION Usually tall, spindly-looking, branching perennial. Stems dark green; sparse foliage means considerable lengths of exposed stem are visible from root to top. Basal leaves long and narrow, with very strongly toothed margins, short-stalked; stem leaves smaller with smooth margins, growing alternately up stem. Flowers a yellow composite like those of Common Dandelion (*below*), more orange in centre but with no obvious point of division between central florets and outer petals; borne singly on stem tips. Composite flower matures into seed head comprising narrow brown seeds topped with fluffy tufts.

DISTRIBUTION Widespread and common across most of Europe, becoming scarce in N Sweden.

LIFE CYCLE AND HABITAT Flowers Jul–Aug. Has fast-spreading roots and can soon dominate suitable areas. Grows in pastures, meadows, woodland verges and on grassy soils close to the sea.

Common Dandelion

■ *Taraxacum officinale* agg. 40cm (height)

DESCRIPTION Rather short, fleshy perennial. Stems smooth, green with yellowish flush, hollow and exuding milky sap when broken. Leaves long, narrow, deeply lobed or pinnate, lobes/leaflets with sharp points; form a dense basal rosette. Flowers a bright yellow composite, with central florets and outer ray petals forming a uniformly dome-shaped feathery head; sepals folded back at base; borne singly on long stem. Forms the familiar 'clock' when fruiting, each small brown seed with a filament and terminal tuft of fluff, less dense than fruiting head of other related plants and often seen with some or most seeds detached.

DISTRIBUTION Found commonly throughout Europe.

LIFE CYCLE AND HABITAT Flowers Apr–Jul. Very familiar and ubiquitous lawn weed, occurring on most nutrient-rich grasslands in town and country.

Common Catsear
■ *Hypochaeris radicata* 40cm (height)

DESCRIPTION Short, slightly branched perennial.
Stems fresh green, rather thin. Leaves similar to those of
Common Dandelion (p. 146) but lobes shallower and with
rounded rather than pointed tips; form a dense basal rosette.
Composite flowers also like those of Dandelion (hence its
alternative common name of False Dandelion), but outer
radiating petals larger, slightly broader and squarer-tipped, less
numerous. Overall composite flower shape flatter on top, and
lacks folded-back sepals of Common Dandelion. Develops
similar seed head to that of Common Dandelion.
DISTRIBUTION Common and widespread across most of
Europe; in Sweden, found in S and extending up coast.
LIFE CYCLE AND HABITAT Flowers Jun–Oct. Grows
in similar habitats to Common Dandelion, although
careful examination of the leaf and flower shapes enables
the 2 species to be separated. Lawns, meadows, pasture,
embankments and other open grassy situations.

Snowdrop
■ *Galanthus nivalis* 20cm (height)

DESCRIPTION Delicate, fleshy, unbranching
perennial. Grows from a bulb. Stems light,
fresh green, fairly slender. Leaves long, slim,
blunt-tipped, similar in colour to stem and
hugging it at base, stalkless and resembling
broad grass blades – 2 leaves grow from base
of each plant. Flowers white, with long
corolla and tight petals; 3 long outer petals
sheltering 3 much shorter, green-tipped
petals; borne singly, nodding on stem;
stamens and stigma not visible. Flower
matures into 3-segmented capsule fruit.
DISTRIBUTION Widespread across most
of Europe; naturalised in many areas.
LIFE CYCLE AND HABITAT Flowers
Feb–Mar. Popular garden flower. Resistant
to cold, flowers often appearing in the midst
of snow or heavy frosts. Woodland clearings,
sheltered riversides and other areas with
rich, damp soils.

Yellow Iris

■ *Iris pseudacorus* 100cm (height)

DESCRIPTION Spectacular tall, unbranched perennial. Stems thick, smooth, sturdy and deep green. Leaves long and narrow, like swords or giant grass blades, with prominent mid-rib and pointed tip. Flowers very large, comprising 3 large, broad, outcurving petals and 3 shorter, upright petals at centre; stigma also resembles a petal; all parts of flower bright yellow, with V-shape of dark spots on each of the large outer petals, pointing towards tips; borne in loose clusters of up to 4. Flower matures into a 3-part capsule fruit.
DISTRIBUTION Widespread and common across most of Europe, reaching as far as central Sweden.
LIFE CYCLE AND HABITAT Flowers May–Jun. Closely associated with wetland habitats, growing at the edges of ponds and lakes, and among reedbeds and marshes.

Lords-and-ladies

■ *Arum maculatum* 40cm (height)

DESCRIPTION Unique perennial. Stems stout, smooth, pale green. Leaves broad, arrowhead-shaped, lustrous and much-veined. Flowers comprise a single large, broad, leaf-like sheath, wrapped up and bulbous at base, and opening out to reveal long brown club-like spike, which releases insect-attracting chemicals – the tiny male and female flowers are hidden within the bulbous base. Leaf sheath falls away and flowers mature into a tall spike of bright red berries atop the stem.
DISTRIBUTION Common and widespread across most of Europe; absent from N Scotland and SW Ireland, and perhaps just reaching the extreme SW of Sweden.
LIFE CYCLE AND HABITAT Flowers Apr–Jun. Insects are trapped in the leaf sheath, where pollen is exchanged. Sheltered, lush places such as woodland clearings, riverbanks, and corners of parks and gardens.

Capillary Thread-moss
■ *Bryum capillare* 2cm (height)

DESCRIPTION Soft, clump-forming, deep green moss. Foliage dense and tufty; at close range, shoots can be seen to form corkscrew shapes; leaves twisted in thick spirals around stems, although straight-leaved examples are sometimes seen. Forms spore capsules, these green, whitish or pinkish pod-shaped vessels nodding on the ends of long, fine filaments.
DISTRIBUTION Very common across most of Europe.
LIFE CYCLE AND HABITAT Grows in clumps or patches on many suitable surfaces. Reproduces via spores, these released from the spore capsules, which form over spring and summer. It grows in rock and stone cracks, on living and fallen trees, and on derelict walls and many other places. It will also grow on bare soil among grasslands, on embankments and on waste ground.

Rough-stalked Feather-moss ■ *Brachythecium rutabulum* 3cm (height)

DESCRIPTION Attractive soft, feathery, light green moss. Leafy shoots are comprised of overlapping, pointed, scale-like egg-shaped leaves, with or without pointed tips, the arrangement on close examination somewhat resembling ears of wheat; shoots are yellow at tips. Spore capsules borne on dimpled stems; capsules and stems both dark brownish, and capsule nodding, oval with pointed tip.

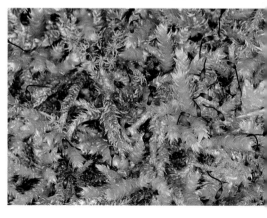

DISTRIBUTION Widespread and common across most of Europe.
LIFE CYCLE AND HABITAT Spore capsules may be observed at any time of year. Prefers damp and shady places; commonest at low altitudes and scarce or absent on highly acidic soils. Grows on dead wood and living trees, on stones and bare ground, alongside rivers and on grass, including lawns.

Silky Wall Feather-moss
■ *Homalothecium sericeum* 3cm (height)

DESCRIPTION Similar to Rough-stalked Feather-moss (p. 149), but with longer, narrower leaves that come to a more obvious sharp, fine point and are borne on long, flat-growing stems with short side-branches. Stems coil upwards and inwards when dried out, but on adding moisture they soon straighten out and also deepen in colour from yellow-green to a rich, fresh green. Spore capsules straight-sided and cylindrical, borne on long, fine stems.

DISTRIBUTION Widespread and common across most of Europe.

LIFE CYCLE AND HABITAT Spore capsules may appear at any time of year. Favours alkaline substrates. Grows readily on limestone rock faces and brick walls, and also on bark of living trees (especially Ash *Fraxinus excelsior* and Elder, p. 116) and dead wood; will form dense carpets.

Wall Screw-moss
■ *Tortula muralis* 1cm (height)

DESCRIPTION Dense, cushion-forming moss. Leaves narrow, tongue-shaped and coming to a fine central point; grow all along shoots. When dry, shoots coil up and whole plant develops a silvery sheen; when wet, spreads out and becomes a rich green. Spore capsules borne on long, fine stems; both capsule and stem dark or reddish brown; capsule stands erect rather than nodding, and is cylindrical, tapering to a point.

DISTRIBUTION Very widespread and common across most of Europe.

LIFE CYCLE AND HABITAT One of the commonest mosses, especially in urban environments. Spore capsules may be seen at any time of year apart from winter. Forms cushions, clumps or patches on all kinds of hard surfaces, including roof tiles, wall cracks, rock faces, tree trunks and wooden buildings.

Crescent-cup Liverwort
■ *Lunularia cruciata*
1.2cm (width of single lobe)

DESCRIPTION Liverworts are simple plants, comprising flat, plate-like, overlapping lobes. This species is a deep, rich green, broad-lobed, glossy, and speckled all over with tiny breathing holes. Lobe edges often very wavy, though shape changes with dryness. Some lobes have C-shaped receptacles containing miniature clones of the plant; these constitute 1 of the 2 ways by which liverworts reproduce, the other being through the creation of spores. Spore capsules appear only very occasionally, and are simple, cross-shaped receptacles.

DISTRIBUTION Very widespread and common across most of Europe, becoming patchy in the far N.

LIFE CYCLE AND HABITAT Favours damp and shady places, often in close proximity to human habitation. Grows at wall bases, among rocks and sometimes on damp lawns. It is also sometimes found growing among greenhouse plants.

Common Liverwort
■ *Marchantia polymorpha*
2cm (width of single lobe)

DESCRIPTION Has larger, narrower lobes than Crescent-cup Liverwort (*above*), with divisions along lobe edges and prominent black midribs down each lobe. Lobes light green, darkening with age. Separate male and female plants, each having disc-like, stalked receptacles with a spreading star of lobes at tip (long and narrow lobes in females, shorter and broader in males).

DISTRIBUTION Patchily distributed throughout most of Europe.

LIFE CYCLE AND HABITAT This liverwort reproduces sexually more regularly than Crescent-cup Liverwort; its male sex cells swim through a film of water on the plant to reach the female receptacles. Almost always found in close proximity to human habitation, and can be a problematic weed in greenhouses and plant nurseries. Prefers damp and sheltered places, but is more versatile than Crescent-cup.

Yellow Scales

▪ *Xanthoria parietina* 8cm (width)

DESCRIPTION Crusty, scaly yellow, yellowish-green or orange-yellow lichen, white underneath. Close up, looks like a collection of small, overlapping leaves or lobes, thicker and more luxuriant in sunny locations. Grows in flattened, usually round patches.
DISTRIBUTION Common across most of Europe.
LIFE CYCLE AND HABITAT May be seen at any time of year. Like other lichens, it is a combination of an alga (a simple plant) and a fungus, growing in intimate and interdependent association to form an organism quite different in function and appearance to either of the 2 component species in isolation. It is probably dispersed by founder cells excreted by soil mites. It grows on wood and, less commonly, on rocks, and may be found in almost any habitat.

Honey Fungus

▪ *Armillaria mellea* 8cm (cap diameter)

DESCRIPTION Develops underground. Produces long-stemmed, round-capped mushrooms, with smooth yellow-brown caps that have darker scales at their centres, and white stems and gills. Stem has a yellow-edged white ring just below where it meets the cap. Grows in very dense clusters, the largest and tallest mushrooms at the centre.
DISTRIBUTION Found throughout Europe.
LIFE CYCLE AND HABITAT Appears from midsummer into late autumn, sprouting at the stumps of deciduous trees or around the bases of living trees. Destructive parasite of woody plants, causing root rot. Infected plants often die back from the top. Common in all wooded environments, including gardens. Spreads by extension of mycelia rather than by spores, so single individual organisms may cover huge areas, producing numerous mushroom clumps.

Stinking Dapperling

■ *Lepiota cristata* 6cm (cap diameter)

DESCRIPTION Develops underground, producing clusters of mushrooms. One of several very similar *Lepiota* mushroom species, and also known as Stinking Parasol. Mushroom stem long, slightly flaky, white or yellowish white. Has a skin-like ring about two-thirds the way up stem, though this quickly disappears with age. Cap broad, dome-shaped at first, overhanging stem, but becoming flatter and eventually concave as it matures; white with dark brown central spot, this breaking up into delicate, light brown-edged white scales. Gills and spores white. Cap fringe wavy. Has a strong, unpleasant metallic smell.
DISTRIBUTION Common and widespread throughout Europe.
LIFE CYCLE AND HABITAT Mushrooms may be seen between Jul and Oct. The species has no specific habitat requirements, and may be found in most environments, including woodland, riversides and gardens.

Parrot Waxcap

■ *Hygrocybe psittacina* 5cm (cap diameter)

DESCRIPTION Develops underground, producing clusters of mushrooms. One of several similar *Hygrocybe* species. Mushroom stem relatively thick, whitish but flushed orange at base and becoming greenish at top. Cap glossy, initially dome-shaped, becoming flatter with age but retaining domed profile at centre. Colour of cap variable but usually eye-catching – may be green, yellowish brown or a deep, rich purplish pink, the colour deepest at centre of cap and fading to whitish at edges. Gills pale, greenish close to stem, large and well spaced. Spores white. Entire mushroom is extremely slimy and difficult to grip.
DISTRIBUTION Common and widespread throughout Europe.
LIFE CYCLE AND HABITAT Mushrooms appear between Aug and Nov. Most often seen in open grassy situations rather than woodlands, including meadows, pastures and lawns.

Brown Rollrim

■ *Paxillus involutus* 15cm (cap diameter)

DESCRIPTION Develops underground, producing small clusters of mushrooms. One of several similar rollrim species. Stem thick, fleshy, light yellow-brown. Gills also yellow-brown, tightly packed, ascending from cap base to cap edges, so cap does not overhang stem. Cap edges thickly rolled under, covering outer edges of gills. From above, cap appears rather flat (slightly convex when young, and gradually becoming concave and funnel-shaped with age) but unevenly so, pale around edges and darkening towards centre, scaly; may show dark bruises. Spores brown.

DISTRIBUTION Widespread and common throughout Europe.

LIFE CYCLE AND HABITAT Mushrooms may be seen between Jul and Nov. They grow under both deciduous and coniferous trees, colonising the tree roots. Woodlands, parks and gardens.

Glistening Inkcap

■ *Coprinus micaceus* 5cm (cap diameter)

DESCRIPTION Develops underground, producing mushrooms in closely packed clusters that may contain dozens of individuals. Immature individuals look like a collection of eggs. Mushroom stem white, rather delicate and slender. Cap oval, becoming dome-shaped, much wider than stem; somewhat transparent (gill partitions visible through it); greyish green, shading to greener at edges and brownish on top, sometimes with distinct brown circular marking. Whole cap has slight dusting of shiny grains, these disappear with age; also becomes darker with age. Cap fringes become shaggier as mushroom matures. Gills and spores black.

DISTRIBUTION Widespread and common throughout Europe.

LIFE CYCLE AND HABITAT Mushrooms appear between Jul and Oct. Grows on rich soil, or on exposed or buried decaying wood; also often found at the base of trees. Woodlands.

Shaggy Inkcap ■ *Coprinus comatus* 10cm (height)

DESCRIPTION Develops underground, producing tall white mushrooms. Grows singly or in small groups. Stem smooth, quite thick and evenly cylindrical. Cap (taking up half of overall height when full sized) also white but may be brown-tinged, oval but becoming cylindrical (overhanging stem), with scaly, flaky texture. As the mushroom matures, cap edges blacken and start to roll up (so cap becomes bell-shaped), and drip a black ink-like fluid that contains the spores. After a day or so it is reduced to a small, flat cap with thickly blackened edges.
DISTRIBUTION Widespread and common across Europe.
LIFE CYCLE AND HABITAT May be seen Jul–Oct. Develops on very well-fertilised soil or on decomposing vegetation. Woodlands, pasture edges, lawns, playing fields, parks and similar habitats.

Coral Spot
■ *Nectria cinnabarina*
3mm (diameter)

DESCRIPTION Develops within the bark of living and freshly felled deciduous trees. Its presence is revealed by the development of tough, rough-edged, cushion-like pink spots on the bark of the tree, which become red as they mature – they may be single or in clusters. These are the fruiting bodies of the fungus, which on close examination are seen to be round with a small central point. They can carpet entire branches of affected trees.

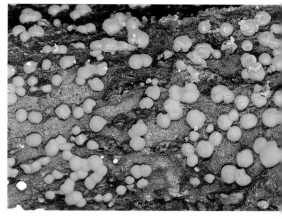

DISTRIBUTION Very common and widespread throughout Europe.
LIFE CYCLE AND HABITAT May be observed at any time of year. It develops on all bark-covered parts of deciduous trees, from the trunk to the finest twigs, and can damage living trees, although it mainly attacks trees already weakened by other infections or mechanical damage. Found wherever deciduous trees grow.

REFERENCES AND FURTHER READING

Bacon, J. (2010). *A Naturalist's Guide to the Mushrooms of Britain and Northern Europe*. Beaufoy Books.
Baines, C. (2009). *How to Make a Wildlife Garden*. Frances Lincoln.
Blamey, M. (2005). *Wild Flowers by Colour*. A&C Black Publishers Ltd.
Chinery, M. (1993). *Collins Guide to the Insects of Britain and Western Europe*. HarperCollins.
Cleave, A. (2010) *A Naturalist's Guide to the Wild Flowers of Britain and Northern Europe*. Beaufoy Books.
Goodfellow, P. (2010). *A Naturalist's Guide to the Birds of Britain and Northern Europe*. Beaufoy Books.
Macdonald, D.W. and Barrett, P. (1993). *Mammals of Britain and Europe*. HarperCollins.
Spohn, M. and Spohn, R. (2008). *Trees of Britain and Europe*. A&C Black Publishers Ltd.

USEFUL ADDRESSES AND CONTACTS

Buglife – The Invertebrate Conservation Trust
First Floor, 90 Bridge Street, Peterborough
PE1 1DY
www.buglife.org.uk
Buglife is the first organisation in Europe devoted to the conservation of all invertebrates. The society undertakes practical conservation, raises public awareness, and supports invertebrate conservation initiatives. Members receive posters, regular newsletters and a free day out with a bug expert.

Plantlife
14 Rollestone Street, Salisbury, Wiltshire
SP1 1DX
www.plantlife.org.uk
Plantlife was established to become an 'RSPB for plants', to champion conservation efforts for plants and fungi in the UK. Members receive the exclusive *Plantlife* magazine three times a year, free access to 23 nature reserves, and invitations to exclusive events.

Royal Horticultural Society (RHS)
80 Vincent Square, London SW1P 2PE
www.rhs.org.uk
The RHS is the UK's leading gardening charity, dedicated to educating the public about good gardening practice through campaigns, courses, scientific study and events. Members get free entry to RHS gardens and discounted tickets to major events like the Chelsea Flower Show, as well as *The Garden* magazine every month.

Royal Society for the Protection of Birds (RSPB)
The Lodge, Sandy, Bedfordshire SG19 2DL
www.rspb.org.uk
The RSPB is the leading wildlife conservation charity in the UK, concentrating on protecting birds, their habitats and all other wildlife. Members help support the organisation's habitat protection, campaigning and research work, and enjoy such benefits as free entry to more than 150 superb nature reserves across the UK.

The Wildlife Trusts
The Kiln, Waterside Mather Road, Newark, Nottinghamshire NG24 1WT
www.wildlifetrusts.org
The Wildlife Trusts work towards ensuring that a rich and diverse flora and fauna thrives in the UK, across all environments, for everyone to enjoy. There are 47 regional trusts, which between them protect 90,000ha of prime wildlife habitat within 2,256 nature reserves. Members can join as many regional trusts as they wish, and in return receive free entry to that trust's reserves and events, among other benefits.

▪ Index ▪

▪ Index ▪

▪ INDEX ▪